The Therapeutic Encounter

The Therapeutic Encounter

A Cross-Modality Approach

David Bott and Pam Howard

Los Angeles | London | New Delhi
Singapore | Washington DC

First published 2012

SAGE Publications Ltd
1 Oliver's Yard
55 City Road
London EC1Y 1SP

SAGE Publications Inc.
2455 Teller Road
Thousand Oaks, California 91320

SAGE Publications India Pvt Ltd
B 1/I 1 Mohan Cooperative Industrial Area
Mathura Road
New Delhi 110 044

SAGE Publications Asia-Pacific Pte Ltd
3 Church Street
#10-04 Samsung Hub
Singapore 049483

Library of Congress Control Number: 2011935041

British Library Cataloguing in Publication data

A catalogue record for this book is available from the British Library

ISBN 978–0-85702–232–5
ISBN 978–0-85702–233–2 (pbk)

Typeset by C&M Digitals (P) Ltd, Chennai, India
Printed by MPG Books Group, Bodmin, Cornwall
Printed on paper from sustainable resources

For our families who gave and give us our place in the world

Contents

Acknowledgements

We wish to thank our colleagues and students at the University of Brighton for their enthusiasm and support for the writing of this book and for providing the context in which these ideas developed. We are indebted to the clients and supervisees who have shared their stories with us. Finally, thanks are due to the excellent editorial team at SAGE for their wisdom and support in bringing this book to publication.

Introduction

This book was born out of an extended and continuing conversation between two psychotherapists from different modalities: one systemic, the other psychoanalytic. Each brought their own professional, cultural and personal experiences as well as their respective knowledge bases. As these collided in conversation and the co-running of training groups, it became clear that what lay between modalities had the potential to enrich what was within them.

David came to the field of counselling and psychotherapy from a background in social theory. He originally undertook a number of humanistic trainings. While much of the learning served to inspire, there was the glaring absence of a satisfactory account of the impact of social arrangements in the training as it was delivered at the time. It is not without relevance to mention the cultural and personal influences of a childhood and young adulthood spent in inner-city South London. The discovery of systemic thinking and practice opened the way to a double coming-home. A full-time training in family therapy at the London University Institute of Psychiatry spent in the Maudsley and Kings College Hospitals took place a short walk from Brixton. At the same time it opened the way to a set of explanations which place individual experience in context. There is a parallel between the rich experience of inhabiting a multi-racial and cross-cultural world and an interest in the way in which theories and models of counselling and psychotherapy manage their differences. David's later professional life as Director of Studies in Counselling and Psychotherapy at the University of Brighton has been given over to thinking and working across modalities.

Heavily influenced by European psychoanalysis, and having been born and raised in Buenos Aires, Pam brought a particular psychoanalytic approach to the conversation. Her relationship with psychoanalysis was initially located within an academic, theoretical frame, and this provided a grounding in psychoanalytic accounts of the tensions between the individual and the social. A passion for early years development led to a clinical training in psychoanalysis at the Guild of Psychotherapists and an in-depth exploration of attachment and object relations theory. Despite this commitment to a psychoanalytic approach, conversations with other modalities have been central to her professional activities and led to teaching on humanistic as well as existential counselling and psychotherapy trainings. A formative experience came during years spent as the Chief Executive of the UK Council for Psychotherapy between 1992–2001. This allowed her to observe first hand the tensions, differences and, crucially, similarities between the then eight

Sections of UKCP at a time when cross-modality agreement was being sought in areas such as training standards, ethical principles and codes of practice. This has provided a commitment to, and respect for, the legitimacy and value of all recognised forms of psychotherapy as well as a belief in the creative potential of cross-modality conversations.

Together with colleagues, the authors have developed an integrated but modality specific training programme at the University of Brighton which allows humanistic and psychodynamic candidates to gain a training in their chosen modality in depth while being in conversation with colleagues in training within a different modality. While orthodoxy and intellectual certainty is challenged, differences are respected and explored. In inviting candidates to think across modalities working with process is privileged.

The book is probably best understood as a series of contradictions. It is intended to assist in the training of therapists but is far from being a training manual. On the contrary, it is against the reduction of practice to methodology. It is about practice but is packed with theory and informed by philosophy. It brings together a number of approaches but does not advocate eclecticism or integration. It is pluralistic but does not propose the kind of pluralism by which a particular therapist is required to have a detailed knowledge of a wide range of modalities, drawing upon them selectively to meet the needs of a given client. It is about resistance but does not accept that clients resist. If there is an underpinning set of principles informing this book, they are to be found in our responses to the experience of being dispatched into the world helpless and incomplete; in the struggles we experience when finding our place in a family and in the wider world. These responses, constructed under desperate circumstances in infancy and childhood, are often at the very heart of our distress as adults. Childhood solutions can become problems in the changed circumstances of later life. Above all, the book is intended to be permissive rather than proscriptive. It does not advocate a particular approach, neither does it set out to suggest that there is a right way to 'do' therapy. In the place of an 'either/or' we propose a 'both/and' position. In doing so, we draw attention to theories and models that inform active intervention through the therapeutic relationship. The therapist is enjoined to be human, spontaneous and creative. We apologise in advance for the deeply paradoxical injunction that you, the reader, should be spontaneous. Equally, we are left in no doubt that you will find a creative way around this.

From our experience it is now a common occurrence in general therapeutic practice for clients to arrive having been 'diagnosed' with depression, anxiety or stress, having been referred for therapy by their GP on the basis that the person will now need support in coping with this diagnosis. There is now a proliferation of anti-depressant and anti-anxiety medication. Culturally, we are in danger of losing interest in *why* people experience psychological suffering, choosing instead to reduce the complexities of a human life to a diagnosis. We then set out to provide either a medical cure or 'learning to cope' strategies. Our psychological ailments are an accident of physiology, it is argued, and we are in need of 'treatment'.

By contrast, in certain therapeutic circles there has been a trend which sees the client given all the responsibility for getting better. As clients we know what we want, it is argued, and need to be empowered to articulate this. Clients are met with therapists prepared to see them as autonomous, rational and self-knowledgeable beings. This is all well and good. However, as anyone who has ever experienced a period of prolonged anxiety or sadness knows: we most often *don't know* what we need or why things have come to be this way. The dawning realisation that we might be unable to manage our relational and emotional world on our own is a humbling experience. Our suffering is often a mystery to us.

So, on the one hand, our culture has encouraged the medicalisation of our affairs of the heart and placed the responsibility for its cures at the hands of knowledgeable doctors and pharmaceutical companies. On the other hand, clients are given all the responsibility for their recovery by therapists who take a position of refusing to know. Yet all of this seems at odds with what we know about the creation of identity, the development of self, and the nature of experience and perception. In Chapter 1 we discuss the prevailing therapeutic developmental narratives which accounts for how we come to be who we are. These accounts all have one thing in common: that to be human means to be in relationship. We find our self through the relationships we have with our intimate and significant others and the messages we get from them about who we are and how we should live our lives. Reality can but be a *shared reality*. Experiences of loss, neglect, rejection, shame and anxiety are borne out of relationships. It follows that responsibility for change needs to lie *between* people. As clients we cannot change on our own, we often do not *consciously* know what we want, nor do we understand the cause of our distress. We do not want *all* the responsibility for change, neither do we want *none* of it. This book aims to explore how a therapeutic relationship might be created in the interest of the healing of one person, but in which two people take an equally active and responsible role. Above all, this book makes a plea for *irrationality* to be given a seat at the table.

A word about conventions of writing. For clarity we refer to the 'therapist' throughout. This can be taken as either counsellor or psychotherapist. The debate concerning the difference between the two can be taken up elsewhere. Randomly, the therapist becomes 'he' or 'she'. This should not be taken as an identification of the authors. When referring to infants, again 'he' or 'she' are used at random. In referring to the 'mother' we are, of course, referring to the primary care-giver of an infant, which may not necessarily be the biological parent. All references to clients and case material are fictitious and have been developed for the purposes of illustration.

Content

Chapter 1: Theorising 'process': contemporary perspectives

This introductory chapter aims to set the scene for understanding therapeutic 'process' as a relational phenomena. We argue that 'resistance' and 'change' can be located *between* client and therapist and are therefore to be understood as a function of their relationship. With this, we set out to make the case for the relevance of what we have to offer to all therapists regardless of modality. The scene is set by providing a brief account of the implications of social constructionism and poststructuralism for the field of counselling and psychotherapy. We argue that these ideas open the way to a climate where, despite commitment to our own modalities, we can value the other. At the same time, we propose that a social constructionist perspective provides valuable insights into the process of the therapeutic encounter. This leads the way to an exploration of the notion of 'self' and 'other' in developmental terms.

Chapters 2–7

Each chapter presents the enactment of a typical dilemma representing a theme of human relatedness within the therapeutic encounter. Working inductively from the dilemma the client is dealing with and the consequent relational invitation to the therapist, principles for productive intervention are proposed. In order to balance the need for depth while drawing on a broad range of theory, each chapter will privilege a particular approach, explaining it in some detail while taking account of others. Proposals for intervention are informed by themes of human growth and development, paying particular attention to the existential challenges faced by each individual: 1) encountering the Self (developing a sense of 'I'); 2) encountering the Other (how we learn to relate); and 3) encountering the World (how we come to find our own unique place in the family, society and culture). Each chapter focuses on the relational aspect of the dynamic played out in the consulting room. Models of change and resistance are linked to specific interventions in relation to each dilemma explored.

In accounting for the similar phenomena, specific modalities draw on different conceptual frameworks. The intention here is to avoid the limitations and constraints which follow from commitment to a given approach. The fluidity of 'personal process' will be privileged over the tendency towards rigidity found in formal accounts of 'personality structure'. Each chapter will be organised around engagement and intervention with a particular client, accompanied by other examples from practice. The models privileged in each chapter could equally be applied to others.

Chapter 2: The refusal to join in

Dilemma: 'How can I take part if I can't make a mistake?'

Here, we have the client who struggles with a sense of imperfection and is all too ready to find fault with the world in general and the therapist in particular. The therapist may well feel criticised and a sense of failure. Developmental models help us make sense of this, and successful intervention requires the therapist to take a position of having nothing to prove or protect while treating invitations to the client to express emotion with some caution. This chapter gives particular attention to psychoanalytic theory, making reference to transference and the Oedipal drama.

Chapter 3: The battle for control

Dilemma: 'How can I find love when I can't show that I'm vulnerable?'

Characteristically, this theme is associated with the client having managed painful losses, rejections and abandonments by becoming heavily defended. The pain and longing for connection is hidden behind an angry exterior. The therapist may well experience the request for help as an attack. Treating fear as information, the therapist is more likely to form a productive engagement if the significance of the client's protective strategies is recognised and respected. Here, we privilege systems thinking, drawing particularly on strategic intervention and the use of therapeutic bind.

Chapter 4: Engaging with the emotionally unavailable

Dilemma: 'How can I get close and still be myself?'

This theme arises out of early experiences of intimacy where the child's expressions of need were met by others who were emotionally unavailable. As a result, the child learns to 'cut off' or negate their emotions and relationships that are felt to be threatening and unsatisfying. The individual presenting for therapy appears disconnected and shows little evidence of distress. The therapist may be lulled into believing that there is no real need for therapy or their interventions appear to make little impact on the client. Successful intervention will depend on the therapist's capacity to see beyond the defence and give a voice to the client's lost internal emotional world. The work of D.W. Winnicott as well as attachment theory provides a way of understanding and working with this dynamic.

Chapter 5: The need to be loved

Dilemma: 'How can keep everyone happy and still get my own needs met?'

A particular child in the family can be 'allocated' the task of keeping others happy or may have played a part in the parental dynamic. As the old story is acted out, the therapist experiences a sense of wellbeing to the point of actually looking forward to the next appointment. It behoves the therapist to recognise the 'seduction' for what it is while remaining warm and inviting the client, to combine the need to be loved with the right to be important. Intervention in this chapter is informed by script theory and the way that the script is maintained in later life.

Chapter 6: An inability to relate

Dilemma: 'How can I get love and still be self-sufficient?'

This theme emerges from early experiences where the need for intimacy has been experienced as a threat to the client either in terms of intrusion or abandonment. The therapist is allocated the role of applauding audience to the client's achievements, wit and intelligence. Intervention will succeed to the extent that the therapist is able to graciously decline the passive position they have been invited to take, connecting with the frightened and lonely toddler hiding behind the desperate performance. Here, we turn to accounts of narcissism to inform intervention.

Chapter 7: Encountering oppositionality

Dilemma: 'How can I get my way when I can't say what I want?'

This speaks to the dilemma of the young child searching for autonomy but subject to adult control. Where control is overly restrictive or punitive, autonomy may become confused with the defeat of the other. This plays out in adult life in self-defeating patterns of behaviour. In the consulting room, the client shows a tendency to do the opposite of what they perceive the therapist requires of them, even if it is not in their own interest. In its more subtle variant, the therapist is lulled into a false sense of security by apparent compliance only to be defeated at the very point of 'therapeutic' success. The therapist will be well served by humour and playfulness combined with a dogged refusal to be organised into 'parental' behaviour. In this chapter particular attention is given to the analysis and management of transactions, drawing upon principles to be found in transactional analysis.

Chapter 8: The therapeutic encounter: a safe emergency

The concluding chapter reviews previous chapters framing the therapeutic encounter as a dramatic event. Persistence and resistance are accounted for by reference to attachment theory, neuro-science and social constructionism. Finally, we consider the implications for psychodynamic and humanistic intervention.

1 Theorising 'Process': Contemporary Perspectives

> Put the emphasis upon a single method of treatment, no matter how diverse the problems which enter the office. Patients who won't behave properly according to the method should be defined as untreatable and abandoned. Once a single method of treatment has proven consistently ineffective, it should never be given up. Those people who attempt variations must be sharply condemned as improperly trained and ignorant of the true nature of the human personality and its disorders.
>
> Jay Haley, 'The art of being a failure as a therapist' (1969)

That you have picked up this book suggests that you have at least a passing interest in therapy. You may be an experienced practitioner, feeling the obligation to put aside reading the proper books that tell you about real life (literature) to engage with yet another account of the therapeutic process. Perhaps you are an enthusiastic trainee eager to learn how to do it from people who have been judged sufficiently 'expert' to convince a publisher that they are worth the risk of a print run. Equally, it is conceivable that you are a customer of therapeutic services – patient or client according to approach – interested in finding out what informs the sometimes puzzling behaviour of the person in whom you are investing your time and, possibly, money. This book is aimed primarily at trainees on counselling and psychotherapy courses, training in any approach whether humanistic, psychodynamic or integrative. However, it is also relevant to practitioners already engaged in therapeutic activity.

Whatever stage you are at in your career as a therapist, you will have made a commitment to a given approach. You will be discovering or know to your cost that this means hours of blood, sweat, toil and, significantly, tears as you engage with a complex literature, attend lectures, face public humiliation in 'workshops' and spent time and money on your own therapy. On the way you will have had to report regularly for supervision where your supervisor has the duty to ensure that you are conducting therapy in the right way (and yours to make sure that you present what you are doing according to the requirements of your modality, disguising or failing to disclose deviations). In short, you have developed or are in the process of developing an epistemology: 'how a person or a group of persons processes information' (Auerswald, 1985). All therapists make sense of what is going on by reference to an explicit or implicit epistemology. As Gregory Bateson (1971) puts it:

> All descriptions are based on theories of how to make descriptions. You cannot claim to have no epistemology. Those who so claim have nothing but a bad epistemology. (p.142)

What you do with the client in an attempt to be helpful – methodology – follows from your chosen or implicit epistemology; 'rules one uses in making sense of the world and how we make sense of others' (Bateson, 1971).

While there are profound philosophical and theoretical differences between counselling and psychotherapy approaches, by their nature they share a common feature. A scene is set within which two or more people meet with a view to achieving a therapeutic outcome. In essence, therapy can be viewed as a series of dramatic events arising from the *encounter* between client and therapist.

Aristotle provides what is possibly the earliest account of the therapeutic process. In the *Poetics* he defines tragedy as the enactment of an action which gives rise to the experience of 'pity' and 'fear' with the purpose of cleansing emotions. Here, of course, he is referring to Catharsis, a notion which has found its way into therapeutic discourse and, though originating with Freud, is most commonly found in the more expressive humanistic approaches. Central to the tragedic experience is the notion of 'harmatia', literally missing the mark in archery. An incident in the plot leads the protagonist on to a path of tragic error and, thus, a noble man is caused to fall by a mistake in his actions. In therapy, the client is both the author and protagonist of his or her own tragedy. The solutions found in the face of the challenges of early experience have led to a life walked in 'tragic error'. That a mistake has been made is hardly surprising since the drama being lived out was written by a six-year-old or even an infant at the age of three.

As therapists, our appreciation of the client's courage in the face of adversity is not enough in itself. We are required to join the protagonist on stage and take an active part in the drama. In this we take the role of 'Deus ex Machina' – literally a 'god out of the machine'. This refers to a plot device much disapproved of by Aristotle (*Poetics*) and, later, Horace (*Ars Poetica*). An inextricable problem in the plot line is resolved by the contrived and unexpected intervention of an outside character or event. Typically a god would be lowered from a crane in order to intervene on behalf of the protagonist. This is taken to be bad form in that it interferes with the unfortunate end that is the proper outcome of tragedy. In the therapeutic encounter it is the therapist who is craned onto the stage in order to interfere with the tragic outcome of the client's drama. But this is not a pantomime and there is no place for a fairy godmother's magic wand. The human condition is far too conflicted and complicated for such simplistic intervention: even good endings are seldom happy and rescuers are asking for trouble. The role of the therapist as deus ex machina is not to simplify the plot but to complicate it. Predicted outcomes are confounded and the way opened for a richer narrative to replace a thin and predictable plot.

To join the drama is essential but insufficient. Once the therapist is part of the performance they are in position to introduce some carefully chosen lines of their own. The system, that is, the complex interrelationships which make up the client's internal and external world, is joined by a polite but unpredictable outsider. The client system has become a therapeutic system and, all being well, nothing will be the same again.

You might want to reflect on this in relation to a client you saw recently. If you are person-centred in orientation, you may have taken the view that the client's difficulties are a function of unhelpful self-perceptions that are restrictive when it comes to achieving their full potential. The psychodynamic reader would have been inclined to focus upon the tasks of early life and tales of repressed desires replayed in a contemporary context, drawing upon the notions of transference and repetition compulsion.

Each of these positions suggests a particular mode of intervention or method: supportive/expressive or transferential/insight. Interestingly, while there are clear differences between each of the above, they share a common 'psychological' position in that: the view is taken that family life shapes personality; the therapeutic goal is changing internal experience; and the vehicle for change is an exclusive relationship with a therapist in a controlled environment.

There is now a convincing body of research into positive outcomes, which privileges the relationship over any particular approach or modality (Wampold, 2001). Importantly, the research also tells us that this is predicated on the practitioner having a coherent framework within which the relationship is understood. As we have seen, there are a number of well-established professional accounts, which have proved their worth in responding to and dealing with human distress. They are to be respected as such. What we are proposing in this book does not require you to give up on your commitment to your approach to therapy and its associated knowledge base.

The position we take is that there are enduring themes in human relatedness arising from human growth and development, family context and social arrangements around which the narratives we live by are constructed. These have relevance across therapeutic differences. Your client brings with them a 'problem saturated story'. This tells of anger, abandonment, hurt, confusion and other forms of human distress providing the content around which the session takes place. Significantly, as the story is told, it is also enacted with the implicit invitation for you to join the drama. What you do next matters. If you take the allocated role and allow the predictable to be re-enacted, you become part of the problem. Each therapeutic model has its own version of how this might be avoided. However, focusing on phenomena which is common to all approaches – narrative and enactment – opens the way to establishing some general principles. These have the potential to enhance intervention making for creative and effective therapy. An openness to new possibilities permits us to benefit from the contribution of: social constructionism; systems theory; communications theory; and pragmatic models for working with resistance. So armed, we are better placed to respond to the predictable with the surprising – the stuff of therapy.

Postmodernism, social constructionism and the drama of therapy

This is first and foremost a book about practice and it is unreasonable to expect the reader to engage with a complex debate which might appear to be several levels of abstraction away from the therapeutic encounter. If you are impatient to get down to business, you may be inclined to engage with other chapters before returning to the philosophical and theoretical underpinnings of the approach. However, in this instance, Kurt Lewin's assertion that 'there is nothing as practical as a good theory' is applicable (1951). That we set out to write and that you are taking the trouble to read this book can be located in what has been called the 'postmodern or linguistic turn'. Traditionally, it might be anticipated that each of us would confine ourselves to the literature associated with our own corner of the field. For some, this might have meant grappling with the demands of the dense and extensive body of knowledge, which comes under the broad heading of 'psychoanalysis' to the exclusion of other potential lenses which might equally shed light on the human condition. Others would have their time cut out directing their efforts towards the abstruse arguments following the latest 'paradigm shift' that the systemic world had inflicted upon itself. Those of a person-centred inclination might find themselves engaged in working out to which 'tribe' they belonged. A new position with regard to the status of theory is proposed; one that is sceptical of claims to truth but has a high regard for knowledge. This opens the way for a climate where, despite a clear commitment to our own modalities, we can value the other.

 Postmodern ideas are slippery and hard to grasp but cannot be ignored since they have had a profound effect upon the field of counselling and psychotherapy. At the same time, we need to keep in mind Best and Kellner's warning:

> The confusion involved in the discourse of the postmodern results from its usage in different fields and disciplines and the fact that most theorists and commentators on postmodern discourse provide definitions and concepts that are at odds with one another and usually undertheorized. (1991, p. 29)

Postmodernism as it relates to therapeutic activity is informed by a conflation or coming together of two distinct but related developments: American social contructionism on the one hand, and French post-structuralism on the other. While the former has had the most direct impact on the activity of therapy, a brief detour into the European philosophical tradition is not without value since it sheds light on some general contemporary pre-occupations in our field. The origins of poststructuralism lie in a post-1968 attempt to challenge enlightenment principles in general and, specifically, the work of Hegel and Marx. The poststructuralists, in effect, turned their back on the grand but flawed enlightenment programme of humanity, progress and freedom in favour of a number of themes, many of which find their origins within the writing of Nietzsche. These are: the rejection of a programme of cumulative and progressive historical change; the celebration of difference over conformity; the privileging of local and irrational knowledge over the universal and objective; moral relativism; and a fascination with the surfaces of things. The relevance of this position to us remains an open question in that there is much that is at odds here with the beliefs and practices which inform helping others. Traditionally, these have tended to look to a secular version of precisely the enlightenment Judaeo-Christian tradition that Nietzschean poststructuralism rejects. However, a number of ideas have significance in relation to what happens in the consulting room.

The first is to be found in a much quoted line by Jean-Francois Lyotard (1979) in his attempt to define 'the postmodern condition'. Lytotard draws on Wittgenstein's notion of 'language game', where Wittgenstein argues that, contrary to common-sense, words do not gain their meaning from their capacity to picture reality but through social interchange. In essence, a language game is a conversation we engage in to determine reality. On this basis, Lyotard declares 'an incredulity towards meta-narratives'. This brings into question the bid by any particular approach to claim supremacy over others. Each modality merely exists within the language by which it is constructed and, as such, there is no basis upon which to privilege one over another. An extension of this is that we are required to give up on the quest to find an over-arching global therapeutic theory, which will finally provide all the answers. Instead, we are required look to the enduring therapeutic narratives which have shown themselves to serve our clients well – a local endeavour. Next, we might take note of Derrida's (1974) familiar proposition: '*Il n'ya pas d'hors texte*' – there is nothing outside of text. This questions the adequacy of language in accounting for the objective world. We are left with interpretation, since language can only ever refer to other language. If this is the case, therapy might be viewed as a process where the client's taken-for-granted linguistic reality is deconstructed, opening the way for new possibilities to be brought into language. Finally, Foucault merits attention. Much of the impetus for the 'postmodern turn' in therapy is derived from what has come to be seen as oppressive 'modernist' practice. Foucault provides a convincing analysis of the implicit power imbalance in the therapist–client relationship – identifying the subtle forms of domination which follow from restricted access to knowledge (1975).

For some, this brief encounter with poststructuralism may have served to frustrate rather than edify. If you are inclined to engage with these ideas at greater depth than the focus of this text allows, you would be well served by Sarup (1993).

The other strand of postmodern thought, social constructionism, has had a profound and direct impact upon therapeutic practice, most significantly in the field of systemic family therapy. These ideas belong to the other side of the world, an ocean away from European preoccupations. They reflect a North American cultural world-view characterised by optimism, openness and pragmatism. The underpinning principles of social constructionism date back to the work of G.H. Mead (1934), subsequently to be developed in the 1960s and 1970s by social theorists like Becker (1963), Goffman (1956) and, notably, Berger and Luckmann (1967). Recently, there has been a resurgence of interest by contemporary thinkers, pre-eminent amongst these is the academic psychologist Kenneth Gergen. There is now an expanding literature which addresses the implications of social construction for the field of counselling and psychotherapy.

According to Mead's theory of symbolic interactionism, the human infant is born with a rudimentary capacity to relate to and adjust to others. Initially, the infant responds to 'gestures' in the form of vocal sounds, movements and facial expressions. Subsequently, the development of language allows for the assimilation of a shared set of mental symbols which, in turn, creates the conditions whereby it is possible for the individual to take symbolically the place or role of the 'other': 'When I am with you I will see myself through your eyes. Further, I will be able to complete mentally your reactions to my actions.' Mead accounts for this process by distinguishing between the 'I' that is unique to the subject and the 'Me', the internalised other. Minded activity, our sense of self, consists of a conversation between the 'I' and the 'Me'. In this way the development of personality can be understood in terms of moving from a 'significant other', the primary care-giver, to the incorporation of a 'generalised other' – the social world. This deceptively straightforward account has profound implications for the way in which we understand the human condition. It presents a direct challenge to our common-sense view of ourselves as boundaried, psychological entities. From a social constructionist perspective, the self does not arise through our exchanges with others. The self *is* our exchanges with others. The contemporary literature in counselling and psychotherapy is littered with references to Berger and Luckmann's classic text *The Social Construction of Reality* (1967). This takes Mead's original position forward, arguing that what we perceive as reality is based on taken-for-granted assumptions. Social arrangements arise from repeated actions, which are passed on to the next generation as social facts.

The relevance of this to our endeavour will have become apparent. From this perspective, the therapeutic relationship can be viewed as an engagement between the client and a potential 'significant other', the therapist. A problematic socially constructed self is exposed to an unfamiliar context where taken-for-granted assumptions are challenged as new possibilities present themselves. So far, so good, but things are not as straightforward as they might at first appear. To understand why, we need to visit the work of Erving Goffman.

Given the focus of this book, Goffman warrants particular attention since his primary concern is with the place of 'performance' in social life. For Goffman (1956), the social world is a stage on which identity is constructed and maintained through a series of dramatic acts. Social life consists of turn-taking, where each of us is actor and audience in turn. We give an 'impression' through the presentation of signals which invite the other to confirm us in our identity or sense of self. For example, on entering the lecture hall, we, the authors, must present ourselves as credible academics. There are inevitably those occasions when we have but a flimsy grasp of some aspect of our material. This presents us with the dilemma of how to convince our audience, the students, that our role as lecturer is legitimate. A strategy is called for. We might confuse the issue by drawing on language to which only the academically initiated have access or we might fall back on easy charm to avoid challenge. Whatever we do, there is an implicit request for the students (audience) to take seriously the impression that we actually possess the attributes we appear to possess. In the absence of this our identity becomes unsustainable or is 'spoiled'. By the same token the students are presenting a complementary performance: taking notes (or doodling), feigning interest and, the brave, asking the odd plausible question. If all goes well and everything goes on as normal, we find ourselves convinced by our reciprocal performances and confirmed in our respective identities.

But things do not always go well. There are contexts where opportunities for constructing a satisfactory identity are severely constrained, and some individuals are disadvantaged when it comes to inviting a satisfactory confirmation of self. We might consider the relevance of this for the therapeutic encounter. In *Asylums* (1961), Goffman uses the term 'total institution' to denote an organisation where sleep, play and work happen in the same place: prisons, psychiatric hospitals, care homes and so on. When faced with the absence of a range of contexts and thus opportunities for establishing a desirable identity, the prisoner/patient/resident must decide whether to enter with enthusiasm into the arrangements by which the organisation functions or to find another way of dealing with an unsatisfactory situation. This is a matter of resourcefulness and subversion, where practices are employed precisely because they are forbidden. The intention is to reserve something of oneself from the clutches of the institution. An accompanying volume, *Stigma* (Goffman, 1963), addresses the dilemma of the individual who is disqualified from full social acceptance by virtue of a discrediting attribute or negative label. This may arise from: a physical disability; a blemish of character; or a tribal stigma associated with race, culture or religion.

There is a world of difference between a total institution and the consulting room but there is, nonetheless, a totalitarian quality to the therapeutic hour. It is intentionally a closed world where only two roles or identities are available: therapist and client. One is desirable, whereas the other has an element of stigma attached to it. We would be fooling ourselves if we did not acknowledge that there is a good feeling attached to the therapeutic role and that there are times when we find ourselves seduced into an idealised persona of the one who bestows wisdom upon the client as luckless supplicant. Therapeutic models set out to provide antidotes to this: remaining congruent; taking a not-knowing position; declining the positive transference; and, most significantly, doing time in the other chair. All that said, there is no getting away from the social construction that being a therapist is a desirable identity (even if we have to put on a disguise at parties to avoid fellow revellers involving us in their problems). The 'client' or, worse still, 'patient' is left with a stigmatised identity and no chance of escaping it for at least 50 minutes. This puts a different complexion on notions like 'identification' and 'resistance'. From this perspective these cease to be properties of the client becoming a function of the therapeutic relationship and the context in which it is located. In your training, you may have become familiar with the phenomena whereby the client starts to take on something of your presentation to the extent of dressing like you, adopting your language and even wanting to train in order to become you. By the same token you will also recognise clients who give every appearance of getting on with things only to sabotage the possibility of any real progress. Despite your best intentions you find yourself looking forward to seeing the former, while the latter are given stigmatising labels like 'passive aggressive'. If these dynamics are allowed to go on undisturbed, nothing therapeutic will happen. Poignantly, both client and therapist are caught in a bind. If the therapist resorts to self-disqualification, the therapeutic relationship will begin to feel unsafe and uncontained. For the client, it will have been bad enough to have come for help without finding that the very context in which it is delivered confirms them in an unsatisfactory sense of self. This is the stage upon which the drama of the therapeutic encounter is set.

As we suggested earlier, the client comes to therapy with a story of human distress. This has been written in conjunction with others and may have been a lifetime in the making. For one reason or another, the story has become unsustainable. The client may have grown tired of the lack of possibilities contained in an impoverished narrative and is in desperate need of new themes and characters. They may have encountered writer's block and are facing the existential terror of the blank page – a nervous breakdown. Relationally, the dramatic performance of the story is failing to convince the audience.

This is where we come in. Our training has entitled us to claim special knowledge about stories. In essence, we have a story about stories in the form of a professional narrative and this can be brought to bear on the situation. We need to be careful about how we do this. There are dangers in the imposition of an established therapeutic account on a client's failing narrative. These need to be addressed regardless of modality. Social constructionist principles would suggest that the therapeutic encounter needs to be understood as a context in which new meanings and their associated narratives can be *co-constructed* by client and therapist.

Writing from a psychoanalytic perspective, Spence and Wallerstein (1982) make the distinction between the search for a 'historical' and 'narrative truth'. The former would have it that there is a factual basis for the client's 'neurosis', whereas a narrative position places meaning at a given place and time. Narratives may be characterised as thin, unchangeable descriptions full of problems imposed upon us by others, or they may be thick with multiple possibilities and full of rich descriptions. To quote John McLeod: 'Therapy is in the business of enabling a client to achieve narrative truth, to create stories they can live by and live with' (1997, p. 86).

As we shall see when we come to script theory, a narrative approach to therapy would have us reviewing earlier attempts at story construction in favour of a richer account that is a better fit with consensual reality and our potential within it.

However, the full implications of social constructionism take us beyond the position that we give meaning to our lives through narrative to one where we *are* the stories we make up about ourselves in conversation with others. As Gergen (1999) has persuasively argued, narrative is not a personal possession. Traditional therapeutic accounts would have it that the client's problem-saturated story is the expression of an internal model of the world, and this is then brought to bear on their dealings with others. By contrast, a social constructionist view suggests that the self is a product of relatedness and is to be found in the space between the individual and others. As we have seen, the story is not limited to spoken language, taking dramatic form as a social performance. This will include non-verbal communication, dress and assorted props. Further, the therapist is no longer an objective observer of the client's process but a co-participant in a shared event.

Family systems theory and the therapeutic dance

Family systems theory provides the theoretical underpinning for work with families and couples. It would be understandable if practitioners who deal solely with individuals were to question its relevance. However, in taking the view that therapeutic encounter is a shared dramatic event, there are a number of ideas and principles within systems theory which have utility. The origins of the principles which underpin the therapeutic application of systems thinking are to be found within developments in mathematics and physics during the late 1940s and 1950s and the attempt to model mechanically aspects of human thinking (Guttman, 1991). At the same time the project for general systems theory was to arrive at functional and structural rules, which could describe all systems. In this process Norbert Wiener (1954) recognised the importance of self-regulation as an aspect of systemic functioning, focusing on the way that information on past performance is fed back into the system, influencing future behaviour. He coined the term 'cybernetics' for the study of this self-correcting feedback process.

Gregory Bateson, working as an anthropologist in the 1950s, is to be credited with recognising the significance of these ideas for the realm of human activity, noting the way in which self-correcting patterns of behaviour are manifest in cultural activities and ceremony. He went on to develop these ideas within the Palo Alto group, which was funded to study communication with particular attention to families with a schizophrenic member. In applying principles from cybernetics to human communication and organisation, this group had enormous influence on the development of family therapy as not just a new mode of treatment but a radically distinct way of thinking and intervening. Bateson, himself, although regarded by many as the founding figure in the development of family systems theory and family therapy, was not primarily interested in therapeutic intervention and subsequently moved on to study communication in porpoises.

The central principle that underpins systems theory is a shift from the taken-for-granted linear view of the world as a matter of cause and effect, in favour of circularity where each cause is at the same time an effect. Cybernetics concerns itself with the way that the output of a system is reintroduced into itself via a feedback loop. Negative feedback will result in stability or homeostasis as deviations are corrected, while positive feedback will lead to disruption and change. The classic example of a negative feedback loop is to be found in the operation of a central heating system where the thermostat 'feeds back' information about heat, turning the boiler on and off to maintain a constant temperature. This may come across as dry and mechanistic but it has significant implications when it comes to the therapeutic encounter. As we shall see, theories of process and resistance can be understood as attempts to counter the homeostatic tendency of the therapist–client system. Salvador Minuchin (1976) has coined the term 'family dance' to provide a metaphor for the intricate way in which family members maintain their positions in relation to one another and deviating family members are brought into line. There is an important caveat here. As Nichols (1987) reminds us, to suggest a family is like a system is a world away from seeing it as a system. The convenience of a metaphor should not be confused with the richness of family life.

Family life is characterised by a series of crises which arise when the developmental needs of members are no longer met by current arrangements. Symptomatic behaviour is understood in the context of crisis avoidance on the part of the family where the tendency towards homeostasis is at the expense of its members' individual needs. This will be particularly evident at the point where a young person is leaving home (Haley, 1980), which can be a time of multiple crises with all generations of family members facing challenging transitions. At the same time that the young person faces the challenges of independence, the parent generation have to re-establish a relationship as a pair and pick up new responsibilities for the grandparental generation who, themselves, may be facing failing health, dependency and death. The situation will be exacerbated if tension in the spouse partnership has been mediated through parenting or where there has been a separation and the young person has assumed a pseudo-spouse role. If transgenerational themes of loss and separation also feature, an intolerable family crisis may be avoided at the expense of the young person concerned through failure or emotional breakdown. In systems terminology, deviation-amplifying events activate feedback mechanisms, which have the potential to affect family life and organisation in one of two ways: either the basic rules and equilibrium of the system are maintained in homeostasis; or there is a dramatic overall change in the rules of the system and a fundamental re-arrangement in the interrelationships between the elements of the system. In this case, the threat to the family status quo presented by the young person's departure can either introduce positive feedback to the family system, taking it forward into a new set of rules and a re-arrangement of relationships, or it can present negative feedback that keeps the family frozen and unable to move on. It follows that systemic intervention is directed towards introducing new information into the system with a view to promoting deviance-amplification in such a way that it cannot be ignored or disqualified.

In the therapeutic encounter, the 'family dance' becomes the 'therapeutic dance'. The client comes to therapy with an open invitation for the therapist to join the dance. This should be graciously accepted. It would be counter-productive to do otherwise, since the dance has been developed over a lifetime and carries with it a heavy investment. There needs to be a note of caution here. What can look like effective therapy can be no more than helping the client to perform old moves with more fluidity and skill. In systems terminology this might be viewed as the therapist being inducted into the system, giving rise to first order change – 'change within the system'. Effective intervention requires that the therapist introduces positive feedback with a view to inducing the crisis that has the potential for 'change of the system'. This may require some nifty and unpredictable moves, not to mention the risk of falling over.

Kenneth Gergen (2008) recounts a story told by the Puerto Rican therapist Egardo Morales about his early days as a therapist:

> He was given a highly difficult case to treat, a young woman with a history of drugs and antisocial behaviour. When she was brought to his office, she sat sullenly before him, her stony face set off with dagger eyes. Egardo began with a congenial greeting and gently outlined how talking together might be helpful to her. She stared silently. After more false starts, Egardo recalled that she had owned a white cat. Abandoning the therapeutic chatter, he asked about the cat. Although the stare was never broken, Egardo did notice a slight movement of her mouth, as if she were ready to speak. Egardo then sat himself behind the desk and began to tell the girl that at night when he was working at his desk, his cat became jealous. He wanted attention. Then, role-playing the cat, Egardo, with a loud *'Meow'*, leaped with all fours on to the desk top. The patient suddenly screamed out, 'You are crazy!' Egardo responded, 'Yes, but I get paid for it.' The girl burst into laughter and with that, an engaging and productive conversation began. (p. 347)

This provides a vivid example of the way in which a therapeutic encounter was creatively transformed from being more of the same to something different. It starts with each participant prepared to engage from the position of the assigned role. The 'passive-aggressive' client, exhibiting all the telltale signs of resistance, is met by the well-meaning and patient therapist. The stage was set for another miserable predictable experience where the client would go away confirmed in her beliefs that 'they' would always let you down, leaving the therapist defeated and disillusioned in the face of yet another client who refuses to be helped.

It follows that at the centre of the therapeutic encounter is the enactment of a story. It is a story so foundational that it provides the blueprint by which the client engages with life. As stated earlier, the position we take is that there are enduring themes of human experience which can be extrapolated from the vast field of human growth and development. These themes constellate around a series of dilemmas, or challenges, which confront the human infant on his journey into adulthood. As the client enters the room and begins a relationship with you, the therapist, he not only begins to tell you about this journey (the problem-saturated story) but he also begins to enact it. This is a story whose origins were written under desperate circumstances. Immature cognitive functioning, helplessness with regard to physiological needs and a fundamental lack of autonomy provide the backdrop against which the infant sets about discovering himself, the other and, in turn, the world. The human infant is, essentially, at the mercy of those in whose care he finds himself and it is from this asymmetrical position that he discovers the world.

The vast body of knowledge that informs our understanding of human growth and development draws largely from the fields of psychoanalysis and developmental psychology. Writers such as Bion, Bowlby, Erikson, Freud, Kohut, Klein, Mahler, Lacan, Rogers, Stern and Winnicott have all offered valuable and insightful accounts of the infant's developmental trajectory. Despite their considerable and important differences, what emerges from this collective body of knowledge is a set of themes which privilege the influence of earliest relationships in the development of the adult personality. The development of a human infant is inextricably linked to his social, emotional and relational world.

Recent years have seen convincing research findings, some from the realm of neuroscience, which have mirrored much of what social scientists have suspected for some time. The 'social construction of the mind' is a familiar notion and one which has been extensively theorised. Contemporary debates around development, however, are having to engage with transdisciplinary discussions regarding what amounts to nothing less than the 'social construction of the brain'. The human infant, born prematurely with regard to neurological development, depends on stimulus from another brain in order to thrive. This has seen a return to the insights of attachment theory, and subsequently the primacy of early relationships in personality development have acquired a broader dimension. The human and natural sciences are now colliding. As if more evidence was needed, these new developments cement the notion that experiences in infancy and childhood are the cornerstone of the adult personality.

These themes privilege the first relationship between baby and primary care-giver as the vehicle for the discovery of, and differentiation between, Self and Other. Furthermore, this primary relationship provides the context from which the infant takes up his place within the social and cultural networks that surround him. The way in which that early relationship is negotiated will inform the manner in which the infant encounters the world.

When one considers the extensive knowledge base informing our contemporary understanding of human growth and development, it is clear that this material is attempting to theorise what could be described as the fundamental questions of the human experience. Who am I? What are other people like? What is my place in the social world? These are the basic existential questions for which the human infant must construct answers. These answers are found within the context of our first intimate relationships and, in this sense, are co-constructed. Human development emerges out of the dialectic between Self and Other.

The very notion of Self, however, merits discussion and exploration. At first glance the concept may appear unproblematic. We are accustomed to referring to 'ourselves' and to other 'selves' in a manner which suggests a certainty about the differentiation between ourself and other people. We have, after all, separate boundaried physical bodies. However, the wish to 'discover' oneself, or the sense that one has 'lost' oneself are, as the therapist reader will recognise, extremely common themes in general therapeutic practice. As we know, individuals will go to great lengths (often distances) to try 'to find' themselves. These phenomenological assertions point to the conclusion that the Self is not a coherent, boundaried and unitary entity which is recognisable, but instead a fluid and changing construct. The Self can be said to be in a process of 'emerging' throughout a lifespan.

The 'postmodern turn', in its social constructionist variant, has pushed the 'Self' squarely into a relational realm. Symbolic interactionism, centred on Mead's notion of the 'I' and the 'Me', Lacan's theorising of the 'mirror phase', and Kohut's development of 'self-psychology' are all examples of how the second half of the 20th century saw differing intellectual knowledge bases converging upon one idea: the Self, in as much as it could ever be known, is located within the intersubjective sphere between Self and Other. The question 'Who am I?', therefore, can only be answered with reference to the Other. Despite their important differences, writers such as Mead, Lacan and Kohut all address the distinction between the Self as subject and the Self as object. It is through relational experiences, mediated by a subjective sense of self, that we are able to construct a view of ourselves as others see us, our 'self as object'.

Our sense of Self, therefore, has evolved throughout our life according to our relational experiences. The event of birth marks the hatching of the baby from inside the mother's body. A separate and psychological 'birth' needs also to be negotiated. Postnatally, mother and baby undergo a subtle, gradual journey of psychic differentiation and it is through this process, this unravelling between Self and Other, that the baby begins to discover himself (Winnicott, 1971). The mother must make space for the infant's new, growing personality to enter the relational space between them.

French psychoanalyst Jacques Lacan theorised the infant's earliest encounter with himself as the 'mirror phase' (1949). In the 'mirror phase', the young infant, who experiences himself as fragmented and uncoordinated, becomes captivated by his reflection in the mirror which provides him with an image of completeness and coherence, which is in contrast to his experience of a disorganised internal world. In a symbolic sense, the mother's eyes and those of significant others provide the 'mirror' through which the infant discovers himself. We find ourselves through the perceptions we imagine others have of us. These will bring with them the weight of all the ambitions, hopes, desires and fantasies our parents had for us prior to our birth (Lacan, 1949).

For child psychoanalyst Donald Winnicott, the discovery of the 'I' is to be found in the intimacies of our earliest relationship. For Winnicott, the mother's capacity to 'hold' her baby symbolises her ability to attune to the baby's needs in such a way that his 'continuity of being' is not interrupted in too traumatic a way. You may well be familiar with Winnicott's notion of the 'good enough mother' who is able to place her infant's needs at the top of her agenda. The 'good enough' mother is able to place her baby at centre stage and contain the infant's anxieties so that they are not too traumatic. Over time, however, she intuitively senses when her infant can tolerate greater levels of frustrations and disappointments (or 'impingements', as Winnicott called them). It is through these moments when the infant's needs are *not* met that he starts to emerge from this state of enmeshment and begins the process of psychic differentiation from his mother. It is these ruptures which provide the opportunity for the infant to see that he and his mother are different separate beings. The pulling away, however, between the baby and his mother is something of a dance which must happen gently, fluidly, with both partners feeling their way. For Winnicott, this dance facilitates, or otherwise, a space into which the infant can bring the 'self' into being. The Winnicottian 'good enough mother' allows her baby to create himself. If, however, she is unable to provide enough containment for her infant, this will confront the baby with his own vulnerability too early. Conversely, and just as importantly, if the mother is unable to provide the baby with increasing space and intuitively 'pull back' enough, the baby will experience a type of psychological suffocation which will leave him equally traumatised. The infant's response in the face of these traumas is to learn to place the mother and her needs at the centre of his story rather than the other way around. This infant will then be preoccupied in getting to know her, at the expense of engaging in the process of getting to know himself (see Chapter 4).

John Bowlby, as the founder of attachment theory in the early 1950s, stressed the formative nature of this relationship with specific reference to the development of the infant's emotional world. Contemporary attachment theory (through writers such as Fonagy and Schore, for example) stresses the function of our earliest attachments as one of 'affect regulation'. This means that the infant learns how to manage his emotional world through the responses he gets from others. Challenging emotions such as anger, fear, jealousy, envy and desire are experienced by the human infant in the context of being part of an 'attachment couple' (Bowlby, 1979, 1988). The responses, or feedback, he receives will shape and mould the manner in which he learns to handle these emotions. Our earliest relationship has taught us to suppress, express, moderate, manipulate or simply cut-off from our extremes of emotions. The key concepts here are that of 'affect regulation' (the mother helping the infant to moderate extremes of emotion) and 'attunement' (the mother's capacity to reflect back to the infant his emotional states). By attuning, the mother helps the infant to understand himself and to begin to regulate his own emotional states for himself (see Chapter 8).

These are some narratives which can shed light onto the answers of the first two questions we raised earlier: Who am I? What are other people like? We might equally have focused on others: Freud, Mahler, Rogers or Stern, for example. They each have their own unique narrative describing the discovery of Self through Other. Now it's time for us to explore the third question we raised earlier: What is my place in the social world?

We would invite you to stop for a moment and consider the answer to this question for yourself, right now. The thoughts that will be percolating through your mind will undoubtedly relate to your current relationships (your role as partner, parent, sibling, offspring, colleague and friend), your current professional standing perhaps, as well as other key demographic issues (your gender, your sexuality, your age, your life stage, your financial standing etc.). Your responses to this question speak to the complex series of social and cultural networks in which you exist. The current status of your professional activities, the politics of the day, the impact of class, the role of men and women in our culture, are but some of the discourses which will be influencing your reaction to our question. In the end, your answer will be a story involving love, power, identity, rivalry, jealousy, hope, desire, pride and pain. The human infant's answer is no different.

As mother and baby begin to move away from each other with the passing of time, the space between them grows and widens. Mother returns to work, perhaps has another baby, and other significant others begin to (re)enter the life of the mother and infant. In short, the baby learns the devastating news, if he's lucky, that he is not all that mother needs or desires: he is not enough. The exclusivity of this seemingly endless first love affair – this most intimate dyad – is shattered. It is from this position – that of a broken heart – that the infant enters the world. The meaning of this heartache, however, is the stuff that will contribute the fundamental plot line of the narrative. Is this a story of unrequited love or one of star-crossed lovers? Is this a bitter divorce or do the partners maintain a secret liaison?

The infant must now take up his place in the social world, informed by the answers to the previous questions regarding Self and Other. Entry into a pre-given set of social and cultural arrangements makes for a puzzling and scary journey into the world. What does it mean to be a girl? A boy? The youngest? The eldest? Who is in charge here? How can I get the best deal for myself? Who are my allies in this family? How do I succeed in getting loved? These are some of the challenges facing the immature and physically vulnerable child. These experiences will further compound, confirm or adapt our notions of who we are (our identity) and what other people are like.

Much like the study of history, the developmental literature suggests that we are bound to repeat our past. Central writers such as Freud, Berne and Bowlby theorise the notion of the compulsion to repeat as being a distinctly human characteristic. Freud suggested we repeat the stories of the past in an attempt to master and process them. Bowlby spoke of 'internal working models' as the expectations of others with which we enter intimate relationships. Recent neuro-scientific studies (for a good summary see Sue Gerhardt, 2004) suggest that we repeat because we are 'hard-wired' to do so – as those aspects of our brains which are dependent on experience are responsible for our capacity to reflect on our feelings and emotions.

In the drama of the therapeutic encounter, a story will be enacted as well as told; scripts will be handed out and roles allocated. Whether what happens next is predictable repetition or the opportunity for a rewriting of the play is the key to effective therapy.

2   The Refusal to Join in

> ❝How can I take part if I
> can't make a mistake?❞

A 40-year-old male client, Tony, arrives for a first session due to recurring bouts of debilitating self-diagnosed depression which last two or three months. During these periods, he can barely get out of bed, let alone go to work and, as a result, is constantly losing his job. Thus far he has been lucky because his girlfriends (of which he has had many) have always taken good care of him and nurse him during these difficult times. The relationships don't tend to end when he's unwell; they tend to do so, quite suddenly, when he recovers from one of his 'episodes'.

During his first session with a psychoanalytic psychotherapist, Tony presents as affable, friendly, but distant. He informs the therapist that he has sought help because his current girlfriend feels that he ought to and, to a lesser extent, because he is frightened of another 'episode' taking place. He is silent but expectant of what will take place. When he asks his therapist what she intends for them to do during the sessions each week, he gets the predictable response. This therapy, she says, does not work like that. There will be no tasks or exercises to do and she does not have a particular agenda for each session. She asks him what he would like to talk about and states that it is up to him to choose the subjects of their conversations. Tony develops an angry tone to his voice, responding that if he knew how to help himself he wouldn't be here and, as he is parting with a not inconsiderable fee, would like to get value for money.

The session goes from bad to worse as a tense silence in the room builds. The therapist has a growing sense of inadequacy, which makes it difficult for her to think about how to recover from what she feels is a very bad start. She finds herself 'explaining' how therapy works and hears herself sounding pompous and authoritative in an attempt to recover her composure. She then embarks on a series of questions which yield little material while Tony responds in a clipped and disengaged manner.

The experienced reader will recognise this scenario as a not uncommon presentation. This type of beginning to a therapeutic relationship can very quickly become a battle of wills: both client and therapist feeling controlled by the other and pushed into roles which neither wishes to take. Consequently, this particular dynamic has the potential to manifest both a 'resistant' client and a 'resistant' therapist. The therapist presumably feels positioned into taking control of the agenda in ways which her training informs her will ultimately be unhelpful to the client. Equally, the client might well be feeling abandoned, angry and frightened in the face of the therapist's unwillingness to either take or be controlled. How did things come to be like this?

Perhaps surprisingly, a second session did take place and indeed a long therapeutic relationship was established. We will hear about how this state of affairs was repaired later in the chapter. Not surprisingly, however, themes of criticism and punishment were central to Tony's story. He had grown up as an only child and was sent to boarding school at the age of eight. Up until then, he had lived in a rural community and, in the absence of siblings, reported having been very attached to his mother. He recalled the decision to send him to boarding school coming as something of a surprise and being sent off very quickly after the news had been broken to him. Even to this date, he did not really understand why this had happened, but consciously rationalised that his father had wanted him to achieve academically to make up for his own lack of education. Secretly, he confessed, he wondered whether his father had thought a boy should toughen up a bit and be 'less glued to his mother's skirt'. His boarding school did not allow him to visit home more than once during the term, and his experience was of his parents essentially 'disappearing' from his life after this time. He had made some attempts early on after his arrival to express his extreme homesickness to his parents. He missed his mother terribly. These had been met with indifference by his father (who always took the calls) and instructions to 'keep his head down' and 'tow the line' for fear that the school might reject him as an unsuitable boarder. His vulnerability made him an easy target and Tony experienced some brutal bullying, learning to manage this by withdrawing from social and extracurricular activities. School, he said, casually, had been a pretty miserable time. Despite his obvious intelligence, he had failed to reach high success and had been a fairly 'average' student. This had further entrenched his sense of 'distance' from his parents.

In the vignette of the first session described above we can see how aspects of this story had been 'performed' by both therapist and client. Between them they constructed a dynamic where both were feeling isolated in the room and experienced the other as withholding and rejecting. Potentially overwhelming feelings of inadequacy could be said to have been experienced by both therapist and client during that first encounter, which might very easily have led to the therapy not getting started. Had this happened, it would have echoed Tony's decision to keep 'his head down' and withdraw from challenging or anxiety provoking situations as a young boy. Once again, a sense of overwhelming inadequacy would have been managed by withdrawal and lack of engagement with others. This enactment undoubtedly pressed some uncomfortable buttons for the therapist as well, as evidenced by her becoming uncharacteristically pompous and authoritative. Any latent sense of inadequacy in her own story will have been activated by this dynamic, as might a neurotic need to prove herself competent and worthy of her role as 'therapist'.

There are a number of developmental models which might help us to make sense of Tony's response to the particular set of family and social arrangements he found himself in. Irrespective of how we might conceptually account for his story, central to Tony's distress is a dilemma: how might he engage with life and pursue his own interests and desires while not risking the criticisms of others or, worse still, incurring brutal punishment?

Undoubtedly there were unresolved feelings of loss and abandonment present in Tony's story which date not only from his eviction from the family home but also from the fact that he had never been afforded any lasting connections with his parents in the first place. Significantly, he found it almost impossible to access any memories prior to the age of eight. What became increasingly apparent in the therapy, however, was his absolute terror of failing or of being seen to be found 'wanting' in any way. As seen in the description of the first session, Tony found it very difficult to be a collaborator in the work, let alone set the agenda.

His bouts of depression could be seen as powerful communications regarding the nature of Tony's internal conflicts. If we take a psychoanalytic approach, Tony's 'symptom' (his depression) can be seen as an unconscious solution to his dilemma. In order to manage the pain of his isolation, abandonment and bullying at school, Tony had developed a number of ways of protecting himself from other people's unpredictable attacks. The question is then posed: What were the episodes of depression allowing him to avoid? What problem were they solving for him?

We will now take a moment to consider some helpful ways of making sense of this puzzle, drawing in this instance from the psychoanalytic tradition. To the non-psychoanalytic practitioner some terms and phrases may seem cryptic or even purposely enigmatic. It is important to stress that psychoanalysis, in its representation of the human condition, has tended to use symbolic language to represent universal aspects of experience. Metaphor is a powerful tool for describing emotional life.

It will perhaps not surprise the reader that the notion of an Oedipal drama may seem relevant here. There are, after all, a number of apparent triangles in this story: mum-dad-Tony, girlfriend-therapist-Tony to name but two. The struggle to find our place in our first triangle, Freud stated, is an inescapable human predicament (Freud, 1924). Contemporary psychoanalytic practice sees Freud's Oedipus Complex as being the manner in which the infant comes to understand his place in the social and cultural networks into which he has been born. The Oedipal dimension is one where the child has to learn, for example, that his mother's love is not exclusive to him and that he must share loved ones with others. He will be excluded from the parental couple and this will give rise to feelings of envy, jealousy and rivalry, yet acting on these feelings will have consequences and give rise to the fear of punishment (Howard, 2008). Thus the internalisation of prohibition, with its subsequent formation of the super-ego (see Box 2.1), provides the cornerstone for a child's entry into culture (Freud, 1930). The Oedipal drama is therefore largely concerned with notions of inclusion and exclusion. Exclusion from the parental couple is the child's first experience of a triangle. The sting from this defeat can be softened if the child is beaten by a kindly and benign victor. However, this is not always the case. The child enters a social world structured and ordered by pre-existing rules and must find a way of managing these while trying to avoid the pain and hurt of rejection and exclusion. Acting on our desires often comes at the price of punishment or rejection from others. Ignoring our desires, however, can be equally devastating, so we find ways, *compromises*, that (at least in phantasy) allow us to *feel* that we are both eating our cake and still having it. In other words, we find disguised ways of avoiding confronting interpersonal conflict, pain or rejection.

Box 2.1   Super-ego

Freud introduced the term 'super-ego' in his famous paper *The Ego and the Id* published in 1923. It is the third psychic agency, together with the Ego and the Id, and acts as an internal judge or censor for the personality. The notion refers to the internalisation of prohibition (of our desires) and of authority (our fear of punishment). As such, its quality is unique and experience-dependent. It represents our own experience of the fear of punishment and the messages we unconsciously received about what our ideal-ego should be. Some of us might have a very punishing super-ego which inhibits our desires and expressions of emotion, while others might feel a distinct lack of inhibition or fear of authority.

Let us return to Tony's story: his experience was that he had been expelled from his family home at a very young age. This had been sudden and brutal and he often felt that this had either been some sort of punishment or that he could not have been worth keeping. His protests of homesickness had been met with further threats from his father of potential expulsion from school. A Freudian account of this state of affairs might suggest that his desires (for the comfort of his mother and his home) had been met with a devastating punishment: being cast out, left to fend for himself against the vicious bullies at school. Tony's Oedipal drama was one where he experienced his parents as being in an impregnable exclusive bond – one which did not allow him any way in. Oedipally speaking, Tony felt that he had very much lost the battle, and we can only guess at the level of anger he would understandably feel at having suffered this fate. A little boy's desire for his mother, we might wonder, was met by a devastating result: the loss not only of his mother's attention, but also of his home and, in essence, his world.

Only a rudimentary knowledge of psychoanalysis is needed for the term 'castration' to be recognised as one that is central to the psychoanalytic therapeutic narrative. As stated earlier, the term 'castration', fortunately, needs to be interpreted very much in a symbolic sense. This important concept merits some reflection, particularly in relation to the case at hand. As the child emerges from a state of fusion with his mother, he arrives at the door of the social and cultural networks into which he has been born. Entry into this club comes at a cost, however, and that cost is that he must become subject to its rules and regulations. These demand that he inhibit, curb and repress certain desires. The imagined punishment for the breaching of these rules is one way of thinking about what psychoanalysis refers to as 'castration'. As humans we all need and want things beyond our own selves, but the world we have been born into will govern what we are allowed to desire.

We will each have our unique relationship to 'authority' and this will determine how forcefully 'authority' will structure our lives. We all know people who operate as if authority really has very little impact on their lives, and yet others for whom those in authority are seen as frightening, inhibiting and punitive characters. Both extremes interfere with the running of our daily lives. For Tony, the notion of authority had been internalised around a trauma, that of his expulsion from the family. In evolutionary terms, to be evicted from the pack is to be left to die alone. How had he survived? Tony had learned to make himself almost invisible – at school, with friends, in his relationships and in his jobs. To be visible was to risk being punished, and to be punished was tantamount to death. In a Freudian sense, Tony might be seen to be in the grips of an 'obsessional neurosis': the obsessional is terrified of acting, thus engages in endless acts of self-sabotage designed to stop himself taking an active part in life. For Freud, obsessionality was borne out of a particular Oedipal constellation where the infant's desire for his mother is met with rejection and the threat of punishment by those in authority (i.e. the father). The child's understandable rage at the inhibiting/punishing father gives rise to unconscious phantasies of wishing him harm or even wishing him dead. In turn, these further enlist the fear of retaliation and punishment from the father, thus immobilising the son from being able to act. For the obsessional to act is to risk severe punishment. In his famous 're-reading' of Freud, French psychoanalyst Jacques Lacan states that the obsessional's predicament is structured around a question, 'Am I dead or alive?' (Fink, 1999). For Tony to feel safe, therefore, he needed to render himself almost dead by not occupying a position as a desiring subject in the world. His was not a fate that could risk the enjoyment of intimacy or professional success as these would bring forth his fear and anxiety and bring on one of his 'episodes'. To act might be to risk punishment by others. When in the grip of one of his 'episodes' Tony felt almost dead, unable to get out of bed and 'live' his life.

During the therapy Tony and his therapist came to see the suddenness of the onset of his episodes as being resonant with the suddenness with which he had been sent to boarding school. He would be sitting at his desk at work and he would suddenly become aware of abusive voices inside his head which would shout obscenities at him (much like the bullies at school). Initially he would wonder if these were the voices of his colleagues. They would then become louder and louder until he would feel compelled to put his work down, grab his coat and leave the premises. He would never return. Without an awareness of his early story, this behaviour may seem inexplicable. In therapy, he came to see this, however, as a re-enactment of the early trauma of being sent away, for having been a 'handful' or, in any case, not lovable enough to keep.

As Freud suggested, the symptom always has a secondary gain, and it is this which makes it the symptom of (unconscious) choice (Freud, 1926). In Tony's case, the depressive episodes, distressing though they were, allowed him to retreat to his bed and be looked after. They afforded him the opportunity to regress to a state of helplessness where he could be looked after in the way that he presumably had longed for as an eight-year-old boy at boarding school. Seen in this light, his depression solved a number of problems: he didn't have to risk failing or punishment at work at the hands of authority figures, he repeated the trauma of eviction from home, and he returned to a regressed state where he could be mothered and looked after. So, if we return to our earlier question 'What problem was the depression solving?', we now have a number of answers: it allowed Tony to escape his terror of authority at work, to rid himself of the anxiety he felt whenever he pursued his desires to be successful, and not to confront his inability to engage in an adult intimate relationship based on mutuality as these too proved too anxiety provoking.

In the therapeutic relationship, the early work was characterised by Tony asking his therapist for 'homework'. He wanted tasks to do and would regularly start the sessions, to his therapist's alarm, with 'What's on the agenda for today?'. When these demands for activities were not met by his therapist, he would become silent and oppositional to the therapist's invitations to explore his feelings, dreams and fantasies. Oppositionality, in fact, became something of a theme between them: either the therapist felt herself being oppositional to his demands to control her, or he felt oppositional towards her attempts to control him. Interestingly, the situation never escalated into conflict as this felt far too dangerous. This 'Mexican stand-off' had the potential to go on indefinitely.

A word about oppositionality: it is a well-known fact that infants learn the word 'no' before learning the word 'yes'. In fact, parents often say 'no' was the first word, or sign, their infants learned (and the word 'more', of course!). The sheer strength or power of those in authority organises the child into having to take an oppositional stance. The constant insatiable demands made by parents ('Put your shoes on!', 'Brush your teeth!', 'Eat your breakfast!') can but be controlled by refusals to comply. The child who is dreamily preoccupied and thus does not put their shoes on, brush their teeth and sits pushing a few cornflakes around on their plate is simply clawing back a little bit of power from within a profoundly asymmetrical dynamic. Tony's refusal to take initiative both at work and now in therapy could be seen as serving a double purpose. It both prevented him from having to risk failure and punishment and also allowed him a certain degree of power, at least in phantasy: the power to refuse to take part. In Chapter 7, we will see how passive oppositionality can thus become a potent and powerful tool and can be seen as a response to being one down. In Tony's case, however, his requests for 'homework' and 'tasks' could be understood as his attempts to control the sessions and to foreclose any possibilities for spontaneity. His therapist's invitations for him to engage creatively with his own story and bring this to life were met by unconscious attempts to kill the sessions off.

Additionally, Tony's girlfriend had 'sent' him to therapy because they had planned to marry. He felt over a barrel – he had to come to therapy or the wedding would be off. In engaging with a new client it is always helpful to give some thought to the process by which he or she arrived at your door. Here a useful distinction can be made between the 'customer' and the 'client'. Ideally, the client is the customer, coming with an investment to engage in the therapy. However, it is far from unusual for the client to be 'sent' by a customer who has an investment in them changing. In these circumstances it is for the therapist to expose the dynamic and seek to form a direct agreement or contract with the client. In the absence of this, the therapy is unlikely to be productive. The customer can be a co-professional who has taken it upon themselves to decide that therapy is indicated without taking full account of the prospective client's views. In this instance, the therapist's first task was to find a way to turn the client into the customer. When asked what it was that he had hoped to get from attending therapy, Tony would respond that his girlfriend was worried that another one of his episodes would come on following their marriage. By the sensitive challenging of the inherent passivity in this reply, Tony, in time, began to be able to give voice to his own terror of experiencing yet one more episode, as during these he would be flooded with suicidal ideation and self-deprecating thoughts about his inability to function in the world. He confessed to having moments of worry that he was going mad.

It is little wonder, therefore, that to let the sessions flow freely and be open to the surprise of the turn their conversations might take felt too dangerous. He found it difficult to start his sessions and made quite pressing demands that his therapist provide both content and the structure. Had she done so, he would inevitably have found these tasks lacking. In other words, in order to prevent his own 'failure' at therapy he was inviting his therapist to fail instead. The therapist was presented with a catch-22 situation: if she gave in to his demands for tasks, she would become the object of his criticisms for failing to provide helpful guidance, but if she didn't, she would be criticised for depriving him of what he wanted from therapy. When the demands came for structuring the therapy sessions with 'activities' it was important that she neither concede nor refuse him.

As was said earlier on in the chapter, this type of presentation for therapy often starts with a battle of wills. The obvious competitive nature in the transaction will not have escaped the reader. Furthermore, we know that Tony's response to competition was, more often than not, to leave the field by having one of his 'episodes'. One might guess here that if the therapist had accepted the transferential invitation (see Box 2.2) and began to over-function, this might, at best, have sabotaged the therapy and, at worst, have brought on one of Tony's depressive episodes.

Box 2.2   Transferential invitation

The phenomena of 'transference' is well known and has been theorised extensively, the term having originated in Freud's famous papers on technique (see Freud, 1912, 1915). The client will attempt to repeat (by way of a performance) aspects of his/her early

(Continued)

(Continued)

relational experience with the therapist. By implication, he/she *transfers* qualities belonging to other previous significant others in their life to the therapist and behaves towards him/her as if he/she possess those qualities. The therapist is unconsciously expected to behave accordingly by the client. This, in essence, sums up the *transferential invitation* which the client will present to his/her therapist. In some of the psychoanalytic literature this phenomena is described as *counter-transference*.

In the vignette of the first session the unprepared therapist initially retreated into a position of 'explaining' how therapy works and, sensing her error, resorted to asking lots of fruitless questions as a defence against her sense of inadequacy. In this type of exchange, the therapist will feel drawn towards one or other of these responses. Either of these, however, would have the effect of colluding with Tony's attempts to 'kill off' the work before it had even begun and would be the antidote to the emotional aliveness that comes with intimacy and connectedness. This type of free-flowing dialectic is not only 'alive' but also has the power of being generative. This was the very potency of which Tony was terrified. The therapist initially found herself working harder and harder to get Tony to begin to explore: this became a competitive exercise where she was asserting that she knew the right way to do therapy. Conversely, this afforded him the position of being dissatisfied with what she was able to offer. This was a cul-de-sac where both therapist and client felt themselves to be inadequate in their respective roles and the pair had succeeded in co-constructing a resistant climate. This was clearly no way to proceed. The task of the therapy in this case might be seen as the opening-up of a space where Tony might begin to mourn what has been lost, explore the anxieties that stop him being able to pursue what it is that he wants and give voice to his buried rage at abandonment. This might, in turn, open the way for him to connect to his desire. How can Tony become curious about his life? To become curious about oneself is to reclaim a sense of authorship over one's own life.

The aim of a first session, it has been said, is simply for there to be a second. This was clearly at risk after their tense beginning. After some reflection (and not too much self-reproach!) the therapist began to see how Tony's defence had served him well. How else would he have survived the brutal boarding school scenario? Consequently, it was important to see that this defence was not going to be given up easily by Tony as it was the one way of being in the world he knew that helped keep anxiety at bay. The resistance which the two of them had co-constructed needed to be subverted, not tackled head-on. Behind this entrenched apathy lay a terror of intimacy, dependency and punishment. The pain of these experiences were so buried that naming them had no effect on Tony – they were met with responses of 'maybe', 'I don't know', 'I don't remember feeling that' and other such bland disqualifying statements. In order for a therapeutic alliance to be made, and maintained, something in the 'performance' in the room, rather than in the 'content' of the discussion, would need to be different.

There are many schools of thought informing how this therapist might intervene in order to move the work on with Tony. A humanistic practitioner might seek to develop a non-judgmental environment through empathy in order to create the right conditions for Tony to begin to tell his story. A systemic therapist would be conscious of joining the system in order to intervene from within it. An object relations psychoanalytic practitioner might very well interpret Tony's resistance as a defence against intimacy. All of these different approaches have been shown to have effective results. They all have one thing in common in that they all have their own way of accounting for the therapist's role being one of not enacting the transferential invitation. This is a tricky business and harder than it seems. The therapist must be reflexive about how the client is positioning her in the relationship and the corresponding emotions that this stirs up. As discussed in Chapter 1, the client's problem-saturated story will not only be told, it will be performed and, as such, the therapist will be allocated her role in the play. To some extent she has to make herself available to join this play, but once on stage, she must play her part in a way which goes surprisingly off-script in order to enrich the story. It goes without saying that she must also consider how the client's story resonates with her own familiar dramas and guard against allowing these to contaminate the process.

The setting-up of a therapeutic alliance requires the therapist to engage the client in a way which makes him feel this is a place where his story will get heard by an other who is benignly disposed towards him. Yet as both research and therapeutic experience inform us, this is clearly not enough. This benign other, the therapist, must also give the message that more of the same is not going to take place in the room. This is not a place where the client will be able to alienate, control or seduce the other in the familiar ways in which they conduct their intimate relationships outside. In other words, a therapeutic alliance might be seen to be formed when the client is (unconsciously) convinced that something different may take place. The therapeutic alliance can be said to be sealed when client and therapist are actively engaged in a joint endeavour characterised by curiosity.

Despite her psychoanalytic training, this therapist chose not to interpret at such an early point in the therapeutic relationship. Tony's dilemma was that he couldn't afford to join in the game of life for fear that he might get things wrong and be punished with rejection and abandonment (again). He managed his sense of own inadequacy by either locating this in others or by not participating at all. In process terms, the therapist needed to show that she did not need to defeat him and, at the same time, was comfortable with her own inadequacy and limitations. She offered Tony an acknowledgement that she really did not know if she would be able to help him. She stated that she couldn't promise to get it right with him and wasn't well versed in 'techniques' for tackling anxiety or depression. She did, however, say that she found his story interesting and could see that he was genuinely in trouble as these 'episodes' were clearly bringing him an extreme amount of distress and stopping him from living his life. She was not in a position to offer certainty and answers because she genuinely didn't have any. His search for these, she said, were reasonable and so she would completely understand if he searched for them elsewhere. What she could offer, however, was a genuine interest in his story and a commitment to its exploration. This had the effect of subverting

Tony's oppositionality as, in the face of the therapist's self-proclaimed imperfection, there was not much now to be oppositional about. As so much of his anxiety was bound up with his fear of 'doing', of taking action in the world, it came as a relief that nothing much in the way of 'doing' was to be asked of him. Neither was anyone else going to be 'doing' something to him. Additionally, by the therapist modelling the acceptance of what she could and could not offer she allowed his feelings of inadequacy to take a back seat. This set the scene for a different type of relationship – one which wasn't governed by the rules of competition – no one had to die here for the other to live and, in time, he came to be able to tolerate both parties being alive at the same time. The tone was thus set for curiosity rather than competition.

3 The Battle for Control

> "How can I find love
> when I can't show that
> I'm vulnerable?"

There was only one catch and that was Catch-22, which specified that a concern
for one's safety in the face of dangers that were real and immediate was the process of a rational mind. Orr was crazy and could be grounded. All he had to do was
ask; and as soon as he did, he would no longer be crazy and would have to fly
more missions. Orr would be crazy to fly more missions and sane if he didn't, but
if he was sane he had to fly them. If he flew them he was crazy and didn't have to;
but if he didn't want to he was sane and had to. Yossarian was moved very deeply
by the absolute simplicity of this clause of Catch-22 and let out a respectful whis-
tle. 'That's some catch, that Catch-22,' Yossarian observed. 'It's the best there is,'
Doc Daneeka agreed.

Joseph Heller, *Catch 22*, 1994[1]

Resistance as relationship

It had been particularly difficult to arrange an initial meeting with Michael. Eventually,
after a number of telephone calls and re-arrangements, he arrived for therapy. Things
started with a complaint about the unsuitability of his chair, one which the therapist
have been using for some years and occupied himself when engaging with couples. The
therapist's systemic training told him that his primary task was to 'join the system' by
establishing a rapport with Michael. It was clear that this was not going to be easy given
his fierce and intimidating presence. Nonetheless, despite the unpromising circumstances, an exposure to humanistic principles organised the therapist into attempting to

---

[1]Reproduced with permission of Curtis Brown, agents for the Heller estate.

offer a warm and accepting response. Throughout the session Michael remained impassive, refusing to make eye-contact and offering no more than the occasional monosyllabic response in the face of his increasingly frantic attempts to establish a 'therapeutic alliance'. There was no doubt about it, the therapist had a highly resistant client on his hands. Fortunately, he eventually got the message and backed off sufficiently for Michael to begin to tell his story. Michael was an only child whose mother had been killed in an accident when he was six years old. His father was unable to look after him and he was taken in with some reluctance by an unmarried aunt. Fortunately, Michael came to the next session. This started with an exchange of chairs and an apology from the therapist for his relentless warmth. The therapy had begun.

For those who have some experience this may be something of a familiar scenario, particularly when working with clients for whom there is a theme of loss, abandonment and rejection. Michael had experienced all three in early childhood. He had lost his mother, been abandoned by his father and rejected by his aunt. Not only this, but in subsequent sessions he reported that he had never felt loved, and we can speculate that the death of his mother served to compound an earlier deficit. We should clarify at this stage that we are not attempting to present a crude causal model which sees early loss as necessarily leading to angry defensiveness. The intention here is to reflect upon ways in which the developing individual begins to construct a view of the world. Here, we are focusing on one possibility among any number. That said, given the kind of life events outlined above, it would not be surprising if Michael had developed a mistrust of relationships. We may take a moment to think about the impact that losing his mother suddenly at the age of six might have had on Michael. Research suggests that the severity of this impact would be determined by his prior relational experience. The quality of Michael's early relationship with his mother would be a determining factor in his capacity to mourn her and cope with her sudden loss. Trauma is not considered to be an external event but rather an internal catastrophe. Michael's palpable anger in the face of any attempts by others to express love and warmth towards him might be seen as a function of his earliest experiences. These ideas point to Michael's internal conflict: he is longing for love and affection but is terrified of betraying this lest these needs are responded to with rejection, or worse, attack.

In Chapter 5 we will be drawing upon ideas coming out of transactional analysis and, specifically, script theory. These provide a framework for understanding the relationship between the conscious and, more significantly, the unconscious 'messages' the child receives from parent figures and the 'decisions' he or she makes about the world on the basis of these. Those coming from a psychodynamic tradition might be thinking about the internalisation of a bad object, while person-centred practitioners would frame this as the development of a self-concept and the formation of a frame of reference. Phenomenologically, what we have here is a theme where the world is perceived as an uncertain and unsafe place where others cannot be trusted. It follows that relationships need to be handled with extreme care since they carry with them a vulnerability to further loss and rejection. In the face of this the best option might be to hide the need for contact behind a presentation of hostility and controlling behaviour. You may have had your own losses and rejections. If so, give yourself a moment to reflect upon the impact that these have had on you and the 'strategy' you adopted in order to manage the pain arising from these experiences. If life has been kinder, consider the child whose life has been characterised by a sense of loss and abandonment. Here, you will recognise the need to guard against further hurt. This moment of empathy is important given the way the 'performance' of this dilemma plays out in the therapeutic encounter. The less experienced therapist and, indeed, any therapist who needs to be liked is presented with a significant challenge, and you will need as much empathy as you can muster in order to respond to displays of anger and criticism constructively. At this point we should include the therapist's contribution to the exchange. Consider your motivation for taking up this work. At a social level this is likely to be accounted for in terms of a wish to pursue a profession where you do something that has meaning, make a difference to the lives of others and so on. At the same time, as you may be aware from your training, there is also a psychological, or some might say 'neurotic', dimension to this. You bring to the therapeutic encounter a childhood dilemma of your own. A common theme for those who enter the helping professions is the continuation in adult life of a special responsibility for the emotional climate of the family in which they grew up and the psychological wellbeing of other members. Here, you might give particular attention to the themes examined in Chapter 5.

The scene is set where the therapist, possibly at an early stage in their career and carrying with them a naive susceptibility to try and make things better for others, encounters a client who proves impervious to these good intentions. Both participants in the therapeutic encounter find themselves engaged in a struggle with very different demons and no possibility of escape for the next 50 minutes. One is organised by an obligation to bring love and affection, while for the other these are a toxic combination which must be resisted at all costs. The therapist, of course, has the responsibility to ensure that something productive happens, but this will not be possible if they meet what they perceive to be the ungrateful client's 'resistance' with fear, anger or avoidance.

You will recall from Chapter 1 that the systemic notion of circularity suggests that in a relationship each cause is also an effect and that the family therapist Salvador Minuchin coined the term 'family dance' in an attempt to capture the complex and interrelated exchanges that make up family life. As we have seen, in the consulting room this becomes a 'therapeutic dance'. The reciprocal nature of the therapeutic exchange brings into question the traditional psychotherapeutic view that places the responsibility for resistance upon the client or patient. This is not to say there are not good reasons for clients to resist. Keep in mind the unattractive identity which goes with being the person who needs help. It is also perfectly reasonable to respond to the unfamiliar and challenging nature of the therapeutic experience with care and even trepidation. The family therapist Lynne Hoffman prefers the term 'persistence' to account for the way in which familiar patterns of behaviour are maintained in uncertain circumstances. This is a helpful idea that we will be developing later. Returning to Michael and his apparently resistant presentation, another framing would have it that this was a legitimate and understandable consequence of the therapist's therapeutic error. The need to make a genuine connection had been supplanted by a 'ritual' of engagement which took no account of Michael's dilemma and reinforced his need to 'persist' in keeping himself safe in the only way he knew how. It will have become increasingly clear that it is not helpful to construe resistance as a property of the client but rather as an action that takes place in context of a relationship (Nichols, 1987). To suggest that Michael was being resistant reifies a process. In effect, he was resisting the pressure for the relationship to be conducted in a particular manner. What we have here is not a resistant client but the co-construction by both the therapist and the client of a resistant context.

This is one in which the therapist and client negotiated their responses to the respective invitations to dance. In this instance, Michael told a story of abandonment and solitary survival. The difficulty in making contact and the complaint about the chair could be viewed as an enactment of Michael's dilemma. The therapist's insistence upon a warm connection created the very circumstances against which Michael had needed to protect himself – love and loss. The stage was set for a fruitless and frustrating process where yet another 'resistant client' refused to be helped. Michael, whose very survival had depended on making a wall around himself, would have infinitely more energy to invest in its maintenance than the therapist, who had an afternoon of clients ahead of him, could ever muster towards its demolition. Another way forward was needed. This took the form of a dramatic moment. The metaphorical loss of control associated with occupying the 'position' of client was acknowledged in the exchange of chairs as was Michael's need to remain in control given potentially threatening circumstances. At the level of content the apology could be seen as an appropriate response to a therapeutic misunderstanding. In terms of process, it served to circumvent what could easily have become a battle of wills.

It will not have escaped the reader that this intervention involved the therapist forming a 'hypothesis' about the therapeutic exchange and setting out to intervene actively. This may come as a challenge, or possibly an irritation, to those practitioners who have adopted a reading of their modality which confuses empowerment of the client with passivity on the part of the therapist. In characteristically provocative fashion, Jay Haley (1976) captures this well:

> Under the influence of psychoanalysis, Rogerian therapy, and psychodynamic therapy generally, the idea developed that the person who does not know what to do and is seeking help should determine what happens in the therapeutic session. (p. 17)

As this discussion progresses, we need to keep in mind our own exchange. In a way the reader and writers are engaged in the very thing we are talking about. We might even call this the 'writer–reader dance' in that there is a relationship going on at this moment, albeit one mediated by and stored upon the printed page. There is every possibility that we have invited your resistance.

Teaching this material to separate groups of psychodynamic and humanistic trainee therapists can prove a dispiriting experience where both groups are annoyed equally. What could be construed as sharing interesting and useful principles can be greeted by accusations of intrusiveness, manipulation and generally being too clever by half. This serves as a very helpful reminder that the therapeutic frame of reference in which practitioners have invested so much time and energy should be treated with respect and care lest we invite resistance.

At this point, there is a danger that this process could be repeated between us and it needs to be reiterated that the established theories and principles that have informed the development of counselling and psychotherapy have served practitioners and the people who come to them in distress well. However, to say this is not to suggest that there are not other possibilities available. Some of them lie embedded in lost aspects of our chosen modalities. Others can be found by crossing the rigid boundaries that tend to grow up around established theories and models. We can be sure that neither Freud nor Rogers would be respectively a 'Freudian' or a 'Rogerian'. The proposal is that we adopt an openness to the creative opportunities available within the therapeutic encounter as distinct from following a series of proscriptions – things the therapist should not do. This tendency is to be found in both humanistic and psychodynamic approaches. Equally, it is present in the determination of systemic practitioners to shake off accusations of 'scientism' and 'user unfriendliness'.

It goes without saying that all effective therapeutic approaches require some kind of active intervention. Psychoanalytic practice is founded upon interpretation; congruence is a central element of the person-centred tradition; and family systems therapists recognise the danger of becoming immobilised as part of the system. Nonetheless, there is a reading of the literature, increasing in its prevalence, which opens the way to therapeutic passivity. Here, psychoanalytic therapy becomes an exercise in withholding; humanistic intervention can take the form of mindless connection; and the 'not knowing' of contemporary systemics is confused with knowing nothing at all.

It is to an aspect of the latter that we now turn. Where humanistic and psychodynamic approaches have shown a tendency to look back to their origins, systemic practice has gone through a series of reinventions or paradigm shifts. You have already encountered social constructionism and post-structuralism in Chapter 1, and contemporary systemic practitioners have turned to these ideas in distancing themselves from what has come to be viewed as the oppression of modernist practice. There have been good reasons for this, not least that the failure to give significant attention to personal experience risks dehumanising the person. In practice, systems intervention brought with it a whole technology of the one-way screen, video camera and earpiece. So armed, teams of 'clever' therapists set out to take on and outwit the 'homeostatic tendency of the family system'. In an effort to become more user friendly, the earlier shift from psyche to system that distinguished family therapy from other modes of intervention has been superseded by another which privileges conversation or discourse. Contemporary systemic practice opens the way for a more human response to the families, couples and individuals who come for help, but it has come at the price of forgetting its own history. We take the position that to argue that earlier systemic thinking has its dangers and limitations is not to say that it is without value. That said, we need to call once again on the forbearance and goodwill of the reader. In the same way that the 'poetic' language of psychoanalysis may have served to irritate some and inspire others, some aspects of the language associated with the systemic attempt to account for the richness of human exchange may tend to alienate. It is worth keeping an open mind since, while they may appear mechanistic in tone, these ideas open the way to exciting and creative therapeutic intervention.

Strategic intervention

Our proposal then is that the therapist takes an active part in the relationship, carrying the responsibility for creating a context where new possibilities are brought to a stuck or resistant therapeutic system. The task is to create a context where something new can happen rather than more of the same. There are some very useful ideas which can help with this, but they need to be retrieved from what has become something of a lost tradition located in a deeply unfashionable end of the therapeutic world – strategic therapy.

In essence, strategic intervention is neither specifically a systemic model for working with families nor a therapeutic approach in general: it is a theory of change. Here, we need to turn to two linked but on the face of it very different therapeutic approaches. First, we have the creative and rather idiosyncratic hypnotic approach of Milton Erikson, brought to a wider world in the writings of Jay Haley, notably in *Uncommon Therapy* (1973). This contains accounts of a series of extraordinary and counter-intuitive interventions and makes for a fascinating read. Despite the attempts to codify this approach by Richard Bandler and John Grinder in the development of neuro-linguistic programming (NLP), Erikson's work has served to inspire and influence rather than to offer a therapeutic approach that can be systematically replicated. With this, there is the work of the Palo Alto Group, referred to in Chapter 1. These are a group of researchers at the Medical Research Institute in California working in the 1950s and 1960s under the guidance of Gregory Bateson including Paul Watzlawick, John Weakland and Don Jackson along with Jay Haley (Bateson, Jackson, Haley, & Weakland, 1956). Their work, which originally set out to develop a theory of schizophrenia, led to the publication of a seminal work, *Pragmatics of Human Communication* (Watzlawick, Beavin, & Jackson, 1967).

Haley defines strategic therapy as any therapy in which the therapist actively designs interventions to fit the problem. For our purposes this may be taking things a bit far, but a critical reading can yield some interesting and useful ideas which have application to conventional therapeutic modalities.

The strategic approach, then, brings together Milton Erickson's paradoxical hypnotic techniques with cybernetics and communication theory, associated initially with Gregory Bateson. As you may recall from Chapter 1, cybernetics concerns itself with the way that feedback on past performance is reintroduced into a system. This can take the form of negative feedback where homeostasis is maintained; remember the classic example of the central heating system where the thermostat set at a certain temperature serves to control the boiler in such a way that it is maintained. By contrast, positive feedback escalates change as each deviation from the norm is amplified into further change. Where the former maintains stability, the latter leads to disruption. When applied to human communication, some very useful ideas come out of this deceptively simple principle of circularity (Watzlawick et al., 1967). These are:

1   It is taken as axiomatic that it is impossible not to communicate in the presence of another. The best we can do is to communicate that we are not communicating. This can be achieved by communicating in a way that disqualifies communication, in other words, irrationally.

2 A distinction is made between digital and analogic communication. Digital communication refers to words and language, the discrete intentional signs attached to particular
   meanings from which we derive information. How this information is to be understood is
   'given' analogically, in other words, portrayed non-verbally. Analogical communication is
   continuous and usually out of awareness. The given and the given-off have the potential
   to confirm or disqualify one another, and the latter has significant consequences for the
   recipient of the information in that to respond to one mode of communication is to be at
   odds with the other.

3 Communicational exchanges are characterised as being either 'symmetrical' or 'complementary'. Symmetrical exchanges generate positive feedback, leading to competition and
   oppositionality. By contrast, complementarity leads to a stable one-up and one-down
   relationship where deviations from the norm are regulated by negative feedback.

4 Change takes two forms: first and second order. First order change serves to restore a
   norm. It is change within a system of relationships in order to maintain more of the same
   when difference happens. Second order change is change of the system, disrupting established arrangements. To return to our earlier metaphor, first order change is maintained by
   the setting on the thermostat. Second order change can be seen as a change of that setting to a new temperature.

To some readers this may come across as reductionist and mechanistic. Bear with us as
we make a case for the value of these apparently dry underpinning principles in making
for creative and effective therapeutic intervention.

At this point, we return to Michael. We have learnt that he has been faced with a terrible abandonment followed by emotional neglect. We can speculate that the 'solution' he
found to these immensely distressing circumstances was to cut himself off and to make a
virtue of his independence. This served to protect him from further hurt. In short, we can
speculate that he has 'decided' to substitute control for love – a 'first order solution' that
has become his problem. Michael might be considered an unlikely candidate for therapy
but we should not under-estimate the longing for closeness that he keeps from awareness.
Michael has been thrown into confusion following an approach from a woman he has
previously considered to be no more than a colleague and for whom he now finds himself
having 'feelings'. This 'feedback' might be regulated by Michael disqualifying his emotional response in some way – a return to the 'norm' of isolation. But he now has an
inkling of the possibility of love. The problem for Michael is that this carries with it a
requirement that he revisit the emotions against which he has worked so hard to protect
himself. The encounter with the therapist, carrying with it the threat of intimacy and the
stress of the unfamiliar associated with the consulting room, requires a return of the old
solution. After his initial failure, the therapist has some success in establishing a therapeutic system by a process of joining and accommodation. Here, the potential for a breakdown in the therapeutic relationship through oppositional symmetricality is managed by
a complementary exchange. There was an apology at the level of language (digital communication). Significantly, this was accompanied by a moment of drama or analogy in
the exchange of chairs. A way was opened to embark upon the shared task of finding a
second-order alternative to Michael's tried, tested and now tired approach to the possibility of closeness with others. Drawing on the hypnotic principles of Milton Erikson,

Bandler and Grinder (1975, 1976) describe this process as 'pacing' and 'leading'. 'Pacing' refers to the process by which the therapist establishes rapport by meeting the client in their own world. This provides the essential basis for subsequently 'leading' them to new experiences. This framing of the therapeutic relationship may be unpalatable to many readers, particularly when it is associated with some of the more specifically hypnotic techniques proposed by NLP, like aping the client's posture and voice tone, matching their breathing and so on. At the same time the validation of the client's frame of reference through reflection and paraphrase, central to the person-centred approach, could be viewed as a kind of pacing. The subsequent insistence on authenticity serves to challenge this attunement, changing the 'pace' and leading the way to a reappraisal of the client's taken-for-granted frame of reference – their self-concept. Psychodynamic practitioners would use different language but would share the view that interpretation will fail without a strong therapeutic alliance. In short, as we have seen, it is necessary to join a system in order to influence it. Towards the end of the session the therapist was at pains to acknowledge how successful Michael had been at protecting himself and offered the view that the wall he had placed around himself deserved appreciation and respect and should be removed with extreme care and certainly not right away. He also offered the view that trust was clearly very important to Michael and that he should exercise some care in deciding if he could trust the therapist. Either way this should not happen too soon.

These closing comments warrant closer examination.

Paradox and the therapeutic bind

In engaging actively within the therapeutic encounter, we are asking ourselves the following questions:

- What is happening or being performed which serves to perpetuate the problem?
- What can be done here and now that might introduce difference?

We have seen that Michael had protected himself behind a wall and is prepared to repel anyone attempting to breach it. Instead of the anticipated assault, the unpredictable happens as the wall or problem becomes the subject of positive comment. You will have already encountered this kind of exchange in Chapter 2 with the recognition that Tony's withdrawal had been the very thing that helped him survive his brutal boarding school. As we have seen, the therapist's initial response to Michael was to inject warmth into the relationship. For Tony a natural way forward might have been for his therapist to encourage closeness. For each, this would be an invitation to the 'more of the same' for which they would both be well-prepared. Instead, the therapist validates the very behaviour that is considered to be the problem. Paradoxically, this has the effect of making a connection since each will feel deeply understood and thus more inclined to lower their defences. The therapist then suggests that Michael not trust him too soon. In order not to trust him, Michael has to trust him and vice-versa. The 'too soon' carries with it the 'suggestion' that there will come a time when he does trust. At this point Michael is in a therapeutic bind, an application of double bind theory to the therapy (see Box 3.1). Some readers may be infuriated by this apparently manipulative behaviour. However, they might also reflect upon implicit paradox in their own modality. It is deeply paradoxical for a client to come for help only for the therapist to insist that they, the client, have the answers. The same might be said of the act of labelling the person who needs help as a 'patient' and resolutely refusing to provide a cure. In reality Michael was never subject to an oppressive logical trap but rather found himself faced with an unfamiliar and intriguing exchange where for a moment he was benignly wrong-footed.

Let us introduce you to another client, Mark. It is now his fourth session and he continues to sit in silence for much of the time, offering the occasional monosyllabic response. If really pressed by the therapist he says something along the lines of: 'Yes, I know that, but how does it make any difference'. We will be meeting Mark again in Chapter 7. The therapist finds himself organised into working harder and harder. At this point something different happens. The therapist confides with Mark that he looks forward to their sessions; that it comes as something of a relief to spend time with him since all his other clients are inclined to tell him painful emotional stories and their constant talking gives him a headache. By contrast his session with Mark makes for a quiet interlude in an otherwise busy day. The intent of this intervention needs be understood in the context of the themes present in Mark's life and, specifically, the experience of punitive controls in childhood that left him with a determination to undermine authority even to his own detriment.

Box 3.1   Double Bind Theory

The principle of the 'double bind' came out of a project set up to study schizophrenia by the Palo Alto Group, led by Gregory Bateson, in the 1950s.

You will have encountered an example of a double bind in the opening quote from Joseph Heller's book *Catch-22*: 'Orr would be crazy to fly more missions and sane if he didn't, but if he was sane he had to fly them.' This communicational paradox underpinned a theory of schizophrenia which attempted to account for symptoms as a function of an impossible communicational system. The conditions leading to 'pathogenic' double bind are:

1   Two or more people are closely connected.
2   A recurrent exchange takes place.
3   There is a negative injunction along the lines of 'Don't do so or I will punish you'.
4   A secondary message which is less direct and often non-verbal gives the message 'If you do not do so-and-so I will punish you'.
5   The victim of the exchange cannot leave the field and is unable to communicate about the communication.

The classic example is the mother who reaches out to her child, telling him she loves him while turning her head away in disgust. The child experiences intense anxiety but

(Continued)

(Continued)

has nowhere else to go and, unable to respond to either message, is left only with the option of communicating that he is not communicating, in other words, by irrational behaviour.

While no longer regarded as a full account of the aetiology of schizophrenia, the notion of the double bind provides a useful insight into understanding how relationships become stuck and distressing. In *Pragmatics of Human Communication*, Watzlawick et al. (1967) use the example of the play *Who's Afraid of Virginia Woolf?* to deconstruct communicational binds the characters place one another in.

As we can see from this chapter, the 'pathogenic' double bind can be turned back on itself to become a 'therapeutic' double bind. Where in a pathogenic double bind it is impossible to win, in the therapeutic version the client cannot lose (Weeks & L'Abate, 1982). Therapy proceeds after forming a relationship characterised by some intensity. The therapist encourages the client in the very behaviour the client wants to change. The client is placed in the double bind of being told to change by remaining the same. If the client resists, there is improvement but to continue with the behaviour is to engage in it voluntarily, and thus exercise control over the symptoms. Put another way, this kind of intervention opens the way from a change *within* a frame of reference to change *of* a frame of reference.

Clients can be encouraged to go slowly in bringing about the changes they are seeking to make, and when there is improvement a relapse might be predicted. We are in the business of helping people move from miserable and unproductive behaviours and experiences to more fulfilled lives. It is only natural that we find ourselves inclined to push and to generate optimism, praising each success. In couple work, some of the best outcomes follow from a declaration on the part of the therapist that the relationship is hopeless. The core intervention in sex therapy revolves around elaborate erotic preparations combined with a ban on actually having sex. The insomniac has tried to sleep, so it is more helpful to suggest that they stay awake. What is being proposed here is that the persistence of the normal and the first-order changes which maintain it can be disrupted by introducing uncertainty and confusion into a resistant therapeutic system. This takes the form of a kind of judo where the means by which the problem is maintained becomes the vehicle for change.

A note of caution is needed here and a reminder that we are not suggesting a 'one size fits all' formulaic approach to therapy. Some general principles are suggested here but it is not enough to identify a 'symptom' and then 'prescribe' it. Each exchange in the therapeutic process should follow from the experience of being with a unique client. Further, this kind of intervention is only appropriate when the client's presentation suggests oppositionality. Compliance would require a very different approach, and there is certainly no place for this kind of intervention where there are issues of safety for the client or others with whom they are in contact.

4   Engaging with the Emotionally Unavailable

"How can I get close and still be myself?"

> Psychotherapy is done in the overlap of two play areas, that of the patient and that of the therapist. If the therapist cannot play, then he is not suitable for the work. If the patient cannot play, then something needs to be done to enable the patient to become able to play, after which psychotherapy may begin.
>
> Donald Winnicott, *Playing and Reality* (1971)

In Chapters 2 and 3 we have seen how two clients, Tony and Michael, struggled to make and maintain connections with others and actively engage in life in ways that were emotionally tolerable, let alone satisfying. Their early relational experiences had brought about overwhelming feelings and, in turn, these had made the proximity of others, as well as following their own desires, problematic and potentially dangerous. The correlation between the psychological proximity of others and our emotional lives is a strong one. The challenge for both Tony's and Michael's therapists was to make psychological contact with their clients in ways which did not overwhelm them or create resistance since, for both of them, intimacy had long-standing associations with acute anxiety and emotional pain.

Each client–therapist couple struggle, at least initially, to find a comfortable degree of psychological proximity. Some clients demand enormous 'closeness' and invite the therapist to have strong maternal or erotic feelings from the start. The work with these clients feels highly charged and there is an abundance of overtly expressed emotion. With other clients, the same therapist may feel that they are walking on egg-shells while intuitively sensing the risk of articulating the unexpressed, latent emotional content of the client's narrative. In these therapeutic relationships, the therapist can feel that 'closeness' is demanded by the client but with very strict conditions: nothing must be challenged. Any attempts by the therapist to encourage a different interpretation of events is rebuffed. Total collusion is required and the therapist must not be separate in any way. Unlike with other clients, the work feels lacking in any energy and the therapist finds himself hunting for signs of emotional pain and distress. The client demands no 'closeness' at all from the therapist and he may well find himself feeling, at best, irritated and, at worst, bored by the lack of connection. It is perhaps helpful to remember that the most disturbed clients are not necessarily the most overtly distressed. These three descriptions are by no means exhaustive and it is not the intention here to 'categorise' people. The point is that with each unique encounter, the concept of what we might call 'psychological proximity' needs to be negotiated and be informed by the particular developmental trajectories of the client and, of course, that of the therapist. How might we come to understand these phenomena?

In Chapter 1 we introduced developmental theories which account for the infant's construction of a sense of self and subsequent entry into the social and cultural world. One commonly held position is that the infant's biological birth does not coincide with his or her psychological birth. This position argues that, as the human brain is born prematurely, we come into the world long before we are able to experience ourselves as thinking, feeling beings, separate from others, and with an identifiably boundaried self. The process of differentiating self from other is a fraught one as it involves the negotiation of dependency and autonomy. The notion of how we come to find the (m)other and discover our self is a key one for helping us understand these different client–therapist presentations.

Child psychoanalyst Donald Winnicott argues that the timing of the experience of separateness from the other is crucial for the infant. He should not have to confront his separateness and therefore helplessness (or the 'me' and the 'not-me' as he puts it) before there is an ego sufficiently robust to manage this anxiety (Winnicott, 1965). For Winnicott, the infant is born in a state of 'un-integration' in which the separation of self and other is not yet conceptualised. There is no awareness of where his body begins and ends. Under favourable relational conditions, what Winnicott describes as the 'good-enough' environment, the infant's continuity of being is allowed to flow relatively uninterrupted. The ensuing sense of calm and its corresponding avoidance of anxiety allow the infant's fledgling ego to develop. When the infant's needs are met, he has no sense of these having been met by someone else, and this process leads to the development of a certain confidence in his ability to remain constant, alive and free from anxiety. Winnicott described this important developmental process as the infant's 'illusion of omnipotence'.

Inevitably, there will be times when the relational environment is such that the infant's seamless continuity of being is brought into question. 'Impingements', as Winnicott called them, will take place and it is essential that they do. It is in these moments that the external world temporarily punctures the infant's illusion of omnipotence and confronts him with his separateness and, ultimately, allows him to discover both himself and the other. This process is a delicate balance. On the one hand, should these impingements be too extreme and/or too early, they might give rise to intolerable anxiety as the infant confronts the existential horror of being utterly dependent on others. Conversely, should the process of separation not be allowed to happen (by a neurotically enmeshed parent, for example), the infant will be stunted in the process of bringing his 'self' into creation and embracing a sense of agency and autonomy in his social world.

The infant–mother couple facilitate a gradual process of the infant's integration of the self. The art of moving apart from the infant at a particular time and pace is a task performed intuitively by the mother in order to bring her infant to psychological life. The steps of this dance cannot be taught but instead were learned during the mother's early infancy and are embedded in her very being. It goes without saying that each mother–infant couple will perform this dance with their own unique rhythm. Before we get carried away with an idyllic image of Fred and Ginger effortlessly gliding across marble floors, let us not forget that most of us have two left feet. For the most part, this dance will comprise a series of jolts, stops and starts, clashes and falls which would not be worthy of any kind of Hollywood performance. The inelegance of the dance will invariably materialise into feelings of anxiety, loss, abandonment, suffocation and, if we're lucky, love.

The psychoanalyst Margaret Mahler, in her famous work *The Psychological Birth of the Human Infant* (Mahler, Pine, & Bergman, 1975), throws further light on this process with her model of separation-individuation between infant and mother. The infant–mother couple emerge into life as a symbiotically enmeshed whole. The couple's first task is one of 'hatching' the infant from this state and enabling him to begin to construct a notion of 'I' as separate from mother. Having discovered himself, the infant begins to explore the world around him and delight in his imagined autonomy and independence. Short excursions are made into the world and the infant begins to 'practise' being a separate, autonomous agent in the world. For those of you who have had the experience of raising toddlers or working with them, you will easily recognise the phenomenon. Toddlers crawl or stumble off to play with toys or other children and revel in their newly found mobility and growing cognitive and motor skills. It's all terribly exciting until a bigger child snatches a spade or a sharp table corner is bashed. Very quickly the joy of going it alone becomes anxiety provoking and the isolation experienced by the infant brings about what Mahler calls a 'rapprochement crisis'. The infant's growing confidence has been challenged and 'an other' is sought in order to restore a state of calm. In most infants this brings about an understandable (and healthy) sense of ambivalence: the infant wants to be reunited with mother and at the same time separate from her. A new way of relating now needs to be found, one which can accommodate closeness but not at the expense of autonomy. Conversely, autonomy needs to be accommodated but not at the expense of closeness. The capacity for intimacy is to be found within the confines of these polarities, and most of us spend our lives ping-ponging between the two.

The 'closeness' demanded by the highly emotional, needy client is often confused with intimacy but, in this model, can be seen as an attempt to recreate enmeshment. With these clients, therapists will find it hard to think, will feel pushed and pulled emotionally, leaving each session feeling drained and exhausted. According to the therapist's own dance of preference he or she may find these clients exhilarating or terrifying. For this client, the experience of going it alone perhaps gave rise to too much anxiety so they collapsed back into enmeshment. More importantly, in infancy there was perhaps a mother who was eagerly willing to return to the symbiotic position. Ultimately, however, the experience of enmeshment and symbiosis begin to feel suffocating for both partners – closeness has been found at the expense of autonomy. These relationships become a battle for survival where one self is sacrificed in order for another to live. The seduction of the breaking down of barriers between self and other very quickly turns into an aggressive taking-over of the other which few can survive and remain feeling sane. This is a matter of life and death. Sessions with such a client may feel enormously cathartic and the therapist may be lulled into believing much 'work' is being done, while nothing of any therapeutic value is in fact taking place. These highly charged sessions are just more of the same and the therapist is simply being recruited to repeat the enmeshment which characterises all of the client's intimate relationships. Any sign of the therapist's psychological separateness will be extremely anxiety provoking as such difference will bring the client in touch with feelings of devastating isolation. The only way to manage the balance between autonomy and closeness is to take the other in (as if devouring) in order to both have contact but remain in control. The therapist needs to work hard to disentangle herself from such intoxicating closeness and begin to think – no mean feat in these cases – about the process that is taking place. The therapist's ability to hold on to her intact sense of self, and create enough psychological distance between therapist and client so that a relationship between two individuals can take place, is the key to work with this client.

When faced with Mahler's 'rapprochement crisis', other infants may have chosen to remain practising. For these, autonomy had to be chosen at the expense of closeness as either there was no one there to return to or that other was so engulfing that to return would have meant a total collapse of autonomy. These infants, it could be argued, have chosen to remain 'practising', or going it alone, in order to survive with a sense of self intact. In adulthood this may present as the person who finds the thought of intimacy with others too threatening as it gives rise to the fear of engulfment and the loss of agency and control. It is not uncommon for these adults to report their partners (if they have any) experiencing them as distant, cold or even 'robot-like'.

If symbiosis masquerades as intimacy, going it alone, or 'practising', is often misrepresented as 'self-sufficiency' or 'self-reliance'. As Winnicott suggested, all we can ever do is move 'towards independence', thus concluding that our relationship to others should be thought of as an 'inter-dependence' between self and other.

Let us meet Liz, a 45-year-old successful advertising creative who presents for therapy following a period of conflict with her female partner. In the first session, she stated that she had come to realise that she had a disturbing lack of empathy towards others, most notably her partner. Her partner had suffered from depression following the death of her father and this had had the effect of making Liz angry and distant towards her. She didn't want to be this kind of person, she said, and knew that this really wasn't a good way to be. She had a big personality, and a very active social life, and found it easy to take centre stage at a party. Her commanding wit made her intimidating and, she confessed, she sometimes used this to put people down. After a few drinks, she might go a bit far, and often had to ring people up the next day to apologise for having been 'slightly out of order' on the previous evening. This worried her. Liz wasn't difficult to like as she was charming, funny and articulate but, her therapist suspected, one wouldn't want to get on her wrong side.

Listening to these presenting issues, the therapist invited Liz to recount aspects of her early life at home with her mother and siblings. Before she proceeded, Liz wanted to know how exactly this therapy was meant to work, specifically she wished to know what role the therapist would play during the sessions. The commencement of therapy was characterised by Liz's endless attempts at rearrangements of sessions as well as demands for very detailed explanations of how therapy was going to work. Liz's professional life (not surprisingly, as we will see) meant that her schedule needed to be flexible when she was working to a deadline, and this impacted on her ability to make and keep appointments for her therapy sessions.

From the therapist's perspective, what seemed clear was that Liz's outward commitment to commencing therapy and attending sessions was at odds with her regular calls announcing cancellations due to other commitments. The three sessions following the first were arranged and rearranged a number of times. Liz's overall concerns regarding these negotiations was that she be allowed to pay for cancelled and rearranged sessions. She was most insistent about this, and her therapist began to wonder about her wish to pay for missed sessions. It was an odd sort of beginning: the setting-up of a therapy process that couldn't quite happen but for which she was adamant that she wanted to pay.

Liz did eventually begin to tell her story. She had an expert command of the English language and her humour had a flowing ease. Her narrative was peppered with self-dismissive remarks about her 'middle-class angst' and she attempted to recruit her therapist into believing that, despite her relational difficulties, not much was really amiss in her world. She often made remarks such as: 'But I imagine that's just normal' or 'You must see far worse'. However, from time to time Liz would stumble upon a memory, almost by surprise, and find herself completely awash with emotion and exploding tears. These moments felt 'other worldly' to her and she would sink her face into both hands.

She had come from a very tightly knit family, the youngest of three siblings. Her father had died when she was only four and her mother had migrated south from the north of England. They had found it hard to integrate themselves into their southern community. Discipline was of the utmost importance in the household and her mother ruled over the family with a rod of iron, both symbolically and literally. She knew that her sexuality would never be accepted by her family and she had been unable to come out to them during her adolescence. Creativity was seen as a threat to the family unit and the young Liz developed a passion for art that was in no way in keeping with the family's working-class values. She was forbidden from pursuing this interest. Rebellions and insubordinations were violently punished, even from a very young age. Liz kept both her sexuality and her artistic talents clandestine for a number of years and, as soon as she was grown up enough, left home and broke all contact with her family.

It was clear that her life project had been one of getting away from her family and keeping secret the aspects of herself that felt alive. Her independence had been hard won and she had been able to leave so young because she had always worked and paid her own way. The performance at the onset of therapy now began to make sense. Liz was not a woman who could afford to reveal aspects of authentic emotional experience to others (hence her anxiety about committing to therapy), nor could she afford to be indebted to anyone (hence her insistence on paying for missed sessions).

The therapist's response was crucial to engaging this client in the work. The constant rearrangements of sessions could be seen as her obvious ambivalence to committing to therapy, which might be taken as a sign of resistance to the work. To return to Mahler for a moment, how is Liz to take the risk of connecting to her therapist and gaining closeness, and still live to tell the tale without compromising her autonomy? The rapprochement crisis which Mahler articulates was perhaps being enacted by her request for therapy but her inability to actually commit to the sessions.

The succession of rearrangements requiring changes to the therapist's schedule could be seen as an unconscious invitation to become parental, even authoritarian. The reader will recognise the feelings of irritation and resentment which can arise in the therapist under this type of provocation. Informed by both their own neurotic structure and their own training modality, therapists will manage this in different ways. On one extreme, some schools of thought advocate a firm approach, encouraging the therapist to 'hold' the boundary and show little, if any, flexibility to the requests. Missed sessions would certainly be billed for from the outset and interpretations made about the resistance displayed and the attacking nature of the client's acting out. Such a response would have the effect of enacting the very scenario that Liz had escaped from in her family. The therapist's 'rigidity' would be construed by Liz as authoritarian and controlling (particularly as the therapist's irritability is bound to leak) and this might be seen by Liz as 'evidence' that therapy (or this therapist at least) was not for her and to quit before she'd even begun. Freud's notion of 'repetition compulsion' is clearly very helpful here (see Chapter 1) as it illustrates how the way in which this therapeutic relationship began was a clear repetition of Liz's earlier life (Freud, 1920). The point is that the therapist is also invited to play his part in the drama: to become cross, irritated, rigid and inflexible about missed appointments. This would create a scenario with strong resonance with Liz's early life experiences from which she'd needed to escape.

Yet other schools of thought might, particularly at this early stage, encourage the therapist to take an understanding and accommodating attitude towards the difficulties Liz was experiencing in attending therapy. The therapist whose attachment pattern tends towards the 'preoccupied' (see Box 4.1) may also find himself leaning in this direction. If we draw on the models outlined above, we can see how this too, while seemingly helpful to Liz's scheduling problems, might create other challenges for Liz. Too-eager a therapist might well be treated with suspicion by this client who has needed to guard against others' wishes to take her over. The therapist is in a no-win situation: to be organised by Liz's constant demands for rearrangements and cancellations would eventually lead to a growing resentment on the part of even the most patient of therapists. This is no way to begin a constructive therapeutic process and, most importantly, would be more of the same for Liz. Her way of managing her terror of connection to others has been to keep them at arms length by adopting a controlling, masterful stance towards them. While she remains autonomous, intimacy does not need to take place.

Box 4.1   Attachment Patterns

Secure

Children with a secure attachment pattern are able to use the mother as a 'secure base' from which to explore the world. The infant will express appropriate anxiety when the mother disappears but is quickly soothed on her return. There is a belief that mother will return and can be trusted to assist in stressful or anxiety provoking situations. The secure infant develops a greater resilience to stress and the mother–infant relationship acts as a building block towards independence and emotional self-regulation.

Anxious-avoidant

The child with an avoidant attachment pattern appears largely unaffected by mother's presence or absence. Little or no emotional response can be discerned about her return following departure. This is often manifested by a literal turning or looking away when the mother greets the child upon her return. In attachment terms, this represents the child's profound denial of his or her realistic emotional need of the mother.

Anxious-preoccupied

This pattern is sometimes also referred to as 'anxious-resistant'. This child is one who finds it difficult to engage in independent play, even in the presence of the mother, and displays high levels of anxiety in the presence of strangers or upon mother's departure. Upon her return, however, the child is difficult to soothe and often 'resists' the mother's affection. This attachment pattern is associated with high levels of expressed stress in the child.

Disorganised

This fourth category was subsequently introduced as it was found that some children did not answer to the descriptions above. These children did not follow a consistent pattern and were associated with a lack of coherence regarding mother–infant separation and reunion behaviours. These children often appeared paralysed or disorientated when responding to contact with their mothers. It is felt that a frightening or frightened mother may paradox the child into an approach-avoidance situation, resulting in freezing or chaotic behaviour.

Equally, to hold the boundary too rigidly could entrench her resistance, as familiar ways of subverting others' attempts at controlling her would be enacted. This would risk the probability that Liz would give up before therapy had even started. Either outcome would mean that Liz's compulsion to repeat her separation-individuation drama would take place. This would constitute a triumph in the objective to repeat, but a disaster in the quest for change. What is the therapist to do? In this case, initially the therapist found himself becoming too accommodating: this had the effect of creating a sense of discomfort in the initial contacts, and a latent aggression/resentment began to seep into these exchanges. Following reflection, the therapist chose to adopt a flexible stance providing it was at no expense or inconvenience to himself. When it was possible to be flexible about dates he was, and when it wasn't he expressed these limitations neutrally – neither with apology nor insistence. This had the effect of subverting the transferential invitation and did not encourage Liz's resistance further. As Liz's motivation for therapy, by her own admission, was her inability to sustain emotional intimacy with others, finding a creative way of making it possible for her to enter and stay in the room was of the utmost importance. In process terms, the therapist was inviting Liz back from her position of 'practising' without having to pay too high a price with regard to her autonomy. She could begin to connect and yet not lose her hard-won sense of independence.

Liz was intelligent and eloquent and this went some way to masking the lack of emotional material present in the room. Intellectual and sometimes humorous conversations could have easily passed the time. Yet, as connections began to appear between her present concerns and her childhood existence, occasional eruptions of raw affect would take place. These were like signposts, flags, to a lost archaic emotional world which had been long buried and left behind. These moments had the quality of surprising archaeological finds which broke up her otherwise coherent account of herself. They invariably related to memories of extreme injustice. These took the form of both psychological and physical abuse at the hands of her mother during her infancy and early childhood. The rhythm of Liz's narrative was one which oscillated between disguise and fleeting moments of exposure. Amongst the least brutal of her memories, Liz recounted how her mother ridiculed her triumphs at art or school and how even minor attempts at self-expression were met with humiliating retorts regarding her 'boastfulness'. These often led to physical punishments. It became clear that a deep sense of shame laced the revelations that came from Liz and which took her by surprise.

The French philosopher Gaston Bachelard describes man as a 'half-open being'; sometimes visible and sometimes hidden (Bachelard, 1958). To connect to the other is to reveal our vulnerabilities and our desires. This was not a luxury that Liz had been afforded, and a pattern of concealment of the self had been set in place like a well-trodden path. A retracing of steps was needed before a fresh relational path could be trod. This was not solely a matter of interpretation: the intelligent Liz didn't take long to understand the route of her difficulties. As any experienced client will report, insight is not enough and it is often the source of much frustration when intellectual understanding does not, in itself, provide the catalyst for change.

A review of the therapeutic literature on shame reveals some interesting findings. Most publications state that shame, and shame-states in both client and therapist, have been grossly overlooked by the counselling and psychotherapy professions. Indeed, Rycroft famously argued that 'shame is the Cinderella of unpleasant emotions, having received much less attention that anxiety, guilt and depression' (1968). Considering the abundance of references to 'shame' in the literature, this is a somewhat puzzling conclusion. There is, in fact, no absence of theoretical material addressing shame, particularly within the psychoanalytic tradition. Why, then, this collectively shared notion that we have 'overlooked shame' within the literature? Perhaps it is because publications on shame tend to focus on theorising the origins of shame and shame-states as emotional experiences and shed very little light on how one actually works with it in the room. Even the very articles that seek to redress the 'lack of attention' paid to shame tend to do little more than to describe its manifestations and origins in childhood. In other words, what has been paid very little attention appears to be the nature of shame as a dramatic enactment within the context of the therapeutic relationship.

Contemporary neuro-psychoanalytic literature suggests that infants are born with the expectation of having shame managed for them. It is a common-sense view that shame plays an important part in the socialisation of the individual. To be considered 'shameless' is not a state of affairs any of us would wish for. Equally, the cringing, burning sensation of shame, and its accompanying paralysis, is one which every human being can identify with. Shame, we might argue, is to be found in the eye of the other. It is our important others who have the power both to shame us and to help us recover from shame-states. Prolonged periods of shame are toxic for the infant's brain and a quick recovery from these unavoidable states is of the utmost importance (Cozolino, 2006). Spend a moment remembering a time when you experienced shame. Notice your physical reactions and any internal sensations. You probably noticed your muscles tense, your eyes look down or close, and your shoulders hunch. If prolonged and unmanaged, shame can lead to a state of paralysis (psychological and physical), intense rage and the psychological and emotional avoidance of others.

Bearing this in mind, it is difficult to see how 'interpreting' or 'analysing' shame, as suggested by the majority of the literature, would have much therapeutic effect. At worst, to be verbally confronted with your 'shame' might have the catastrophic effect of having the experience compounded. If shame is in the eye of the other (either real or internalised), then only the other has the power to detoxify this experience. The perception that we have failed to address the question of shame speaks to the very heart of the privacy of the consulting room. Now spend a moment thinking about the last time you saw someone else in a state of shame. Perhaps this was at a lecture when someone lost their train of thought, or nerves got the better of them, or perhaps it was an image in a film portraying someone being subjected to some form of humiliation or debasement. What does it feel like to witness another's shame? Extreme discomfort and an urge to look away appear to be central to these human experiences. To really connect with someone in a state of shame is to risk confronting something quite frightening in ourselves. There is a fine line between empathy and identification, and no-one wants to be reminded of this most abject of experiences.

The therapeutic other, in his role of benign witness, is the one who holds the power to detoxify the shame of the client. Having the tenacity to stay close to the client's material, not to rescue or reframe, the therapist must overcome his urge to symbolically look away or to move things on too fast. To witness the other's shame, experience it and then guide the way to a more accepting place, is to model the type of recovery from shame-states on which infants rely. This is not something we human beings can do on our own. It was essential that in her fleeting moments of self-revelation, Liz was met neither by silence nor by interpretation, but by a human connection which showed a containing understanding of the horror of these feelings. These were dramatic re-engagements with her shameful experiences, but ones which could be re-lived relationally to a different ending.

Due to her work schedule, Liz came and went from therapy. She would attend regularly for a while and then be unable to attend for periods of time when 'things got very busy'. While these were of course real commitments, it was no coincidence that she had set her life up this way. One might take the view that her unorthodox departures from therapy were defensive and evidence of her resistance to engage with the work: no doubt they were, but to stop there was not to see the whole story. Liz and her therapist began to see these ruptures as attempts to work something through. Could she depart and still return? Could she return from 'practising' and be met by an other who would not reject or engulf her? In time her resilience to intimacy strengthened and she could tolerate longer periods of time in connection while in the relative safety of the therapeutic relationship. For her therapist, what became apparent was that the degree of 'psychological proximity' began to shift and the distance in the room narrowed.

Her need to depart was both about withdrawing and about creating the conditions under which she might return and, in this sense, her dramatic re-enactment was paradoxical. For her therapist, allowing her the freedom to come and go while making it known to her that her therapy was important and worthwhile was a difficult balance to strike, but essential in the quest for making intimacy a real possibility. Escaping had been Liz's means of survival; it was what had kept her psychologically alive. In managing this tension, it was important to acknowledge that what might be termed her 'defence' had been the key to her success. Her ability to cut off from others and ruthlessly pursue her self-interests had ensured her survival, but had left her desperately isolated from others. Much like Michael in Chapter 3, the therapist had to both accept Liz's need to keep him distant and insist on giving voice to Liz's emotional pain. In other words, the therapist allowed Liz the possibility of having her needs met without needing to surrender her hard-won independence.

At the time of coming to therapy, however, Liz was experiencing something of a 'block' to her ability to be creative at work and she was puzzled by this. Turning to 'attachment theory' might be one more way of understanding Liz's difficulties. Most informed readers will be familiar with the fundamentals of this model. Experiences of our earliest attachments become organised into patterns, 'internal working models' as Bowlby called them, which can be thought of as lenses through which to see the world. These patterns act like blueprints for the relationships we seek and the dynamics we unconsciously orchestrate. Attachment theory draws on the pioneering work of John Bowlby and his follower, Mary Ainsworth (Ainsworth & Bowlby, 1965; Ainsworth, 1967), and also on more contemporary thinkers and writers such as Peter Fonagy and Mary Targett amongst others (for a description of attachment patterns see Box 4.1). While seeing clients through the lense of attachment patterns is perhaps a little two-dimensional, these are helpful 'short-cuts' for grasping how the client is managing the economics of their emotions.

The reader will notice that each of the attachment patterns described in Box 4.1 refer to the infant's strategy for managing stress. In the small percentage of infants who would fit the 'disorganised' attachment pattern, what we see is the absence of a strategy for the management of stress. This tends to be associated with stories of abuse and/or relational trauma. The strategies for managing stress employed by the infants in the other three categories are developed between mother and infant. Infants are not born with the capacity to manage stress independently, and their immature cognitive and physical abilities means that the world can be a pretty frightening place. How the mother–infant couple learn together to manage not only the infant's stress but also his or her anger, frustration and desire, is referred to in the attachment literature as 'affect-regulation'. We can deduce that the secure infant has had the experience of having their stress managed for them and that the mother has been available to both soothe and temper the child's anxiety and frustration. This is not only about empathy but about boundaries as well. If the infant's expression of anger and frustration are met by either cold withdrawal or too punitive a response, then the message the infant receives is that it is not safe to express such emotions and that these confrontations are best avoided. Equally, if when the infant is stressed or anxious they see a mother who too becomes stressed, anxious and unable to control these in herself, the message they are receiving is that stress has the potential to overwhelm them. This might well give rise to fantasies of total collapse and escalate into feelings of panic. Put simply, an 'avoidant infant' is one who has had to learn to cut off from expressing their emotions and has learned to deny their need of others. For an infant to behave as if mother's absence is an irrelevance is a denial of colossal proportions. The pre-occupied infant and his mother, by contrast, have developed a pattern where the infant needs to amplify his or her feelings of stress because there is no internalised belief that this will be contained for them and thus they are easily overwhelmed.

The problem with categorising individuals in the way suggested by attachment theory is that these categories can encourage a type of simplistic correlation between what might be called 'symptoms' (e.g. 'being avoidant') with their underlying meaning. No two securely attached infants will have had the same experiences. So too each individual who answers to the description of being avoidant will have arrived at this position as a result of their own unique complex and idiosyncratic narrative. The specificity of their story will be the key to understanding the meaning of their own particular relational dilemma. What matters is less the type of attachment pattern the therapist might discern in their client, but rather the unique journey which has been undertaken by the client.

Nevertheless, in this model there could be little doubt that Liz presented with clear signs of an avoidant attachment pattern. While she was engaging and commanding, Liz had very low levels of emotional expression and was not a woman who could be easily reached. She described her inability to empathise with others, which kept her isolated from people. For Liz, avoidance had become a way of being in order to keep the more authentic aspects of herself safe from shame and rejection. Isolation (masking as autonomy) was a logical choice under such conditions. Logical perhaps, but a block to creativity. As Winnicott argued, to be creative from within the self, the world and others in it must be let in. In turn, the encountering of the other in intimacy requires the experiencing and surviving of challenging emotional situations. Intimacy requires us to give voice to our desires and these in turn put us in touch with jealousy, envy, anxiety, anger, love and lust. We cut off from these emotions at our peril – to be blind to our internal emotional life is to lose contact with our desire. In Liz's absence of emotional connection to others, her internal well of creativity had dried up. To reconnect with herself, others would need to be let in. Through shame's brute force, she had been asked to give up her own identity in order to gain the acceptance of others. This was not a price that Liz had been prepared to pay. In time, and with her therapist's encouragement, these new experiences enacted in therapy could be exported into Liz's intimate life. She could begin to risk revealing aspects of herself to her partner and friends in ways that opened the way to a new mutuality.

5   The Need to be Loved

> **"**How can I keep
> everyone happy and still
> get my own needs met?**"**

Does not Dionysius seem to have declared that there can be no happiness for
one who is under constant apprehension?

Cicero's *Tusculan Disputations*. 5 (translated C.D. Jonge, 1817, p. 185)

As we have seen, the client arrives at the therapist's consulting room with a presenting problem which needs to be understood against the background of a story about the world constructed in conjunction with others in early childhood and played out over a lifetime. The therapist's task is to bring to bear their therapeutic account about such stories with a view to co-constructing new possibilities in the place of the client's failing narrative. We have argued that a central aspect of therapeutic intervention involves a dramatic re-enactment of the childhood story but one in which the therapist allows him- or herself to be inducted into the drama with a view, subsequently, to engender an unpredicted outcome. Here, we turn to the valuable contribution that transactional analysis (TA) can bring to our understanding of this process. First, a word of warning to those who have not encountered this approach before or who have only a cursory knowledge. Experience of teaching this material suggests that those from a psychoanalytic background are inclined to dismiss it as 'Mickey Mouse' Freud, while proponents of the person-centred approach are offended by what they regard as a tendency to over-theorise in a knowing way. This is compounded by the misapplication of TA principles in sales and management training along with an annoying tendency of a certain kind of practitioner to name 'games' while making reference to how their 'Child' has been hurt. An unfortunate consequence of Berne's laudable attempt to make theory accessible to clients in order to enlist them as active participants in their own therapy has been the use of what now can come across as rather dated and Americanised terminology. In this Chapter, the reader will encounter a number of concepts in unfamiliar language: 'games', 'rackets', 'drivers', 'scripts', 'the drama triangle' and 'discounting'. While those with some initial training in TA will be familiar with this kind of terminology, it may be off-putting to readers less familiar with the approach. Here, you might find it helpful to refer to Ian Stewart and Vann Joines' excellent overview in *TA Today* (1987).

Eric Berne, the originator of the approach, achieved something remarkable. Coming from a psychoanalytic background, he managed to synthesise ideas and principles from a number of approaches. TA is: psychodynamic in that it accounts for the intra-psychic interaction; systemic in the analysis of transactions and 'games'; existential-phenomenological through an emphasis on personal responsibility; and, significantly for our purposes, it brings narrative and drama to the therapeutic exchange, referring specifically to the notion of 'script'.

The origins of TA, alongside client-centred therapy and gestalt therapy, can be located within the so-called 'new psychotherapies' developed on the West Coast of America in the post-war period as a reaction to the dominance of psychoanalysis and behaviourism in America at the time.

To return to practice; imagine this scene:

It is a cold November morning. You drag yourself out of bed struggling with a reluctance to make your way to your consulting room for the first appointment of the day. As you leave home, your head clears and you recall that you are due to see Lucy. Unaccountably, your mood lifts and you develop a spring in your step as you reflect upon your brilliant interventions in the last session and how appreciative Lucy had been. Leaning towards you, a brave half smile on her face, her large blues eyes wide-open in admiration, she had confided that, compared with you, her previous therapist had been something of a disappointment. As she left at the end of the session, slightly early because she had taken up enough of your time already, you found yourself glowing with a sense of achievement. This had been a marked contrast with the sense of frustration and inadequacy that characterised your work with other clients that day.

On reflection, possibly in supervision, you will no doubt have come to the realisation that, while your response to Lucy was important information, it was not to be taken as an indication that you were doing well. Here, you might refer back to Box 2.2, transferential invitation. For the purposes of this chapter we will bring a TA perspective to this dynamic drawing particularly on script theory.

Used in this context, the notion of script connects adult functioning with experiences in early life. The previous chapter provided an account of the significance of the parent–child bond and the implications of this for subsequent relationships. In script theory, this phenomenon is framed in terms of 'decisions' made by the child in response to the 'messages' they receive from care-givers. In essence, the young infant constructs a life-plan on the basis of decisions arrived at from the manner in which they are handled and responded to in early life, that is, the messages they receive about the world. This is a matter of survival, as the child attempts to ensure that their needs are met in what might appear to them to be a hostile and uncertain context. Here, we need to bear in mind that the earliest and arguably the most powerful decisions are without the benefit of mature thinking and will have an irrational or magical quality to them. Over time, these early constructions are developed and form the basis of a consistent and taken-for-granted frame of reference. In later life the way in which an individual relates will be consistent with and reinforcing of their script beliefs about others and the world. Further, aspects of experience which are at odds with these beliefs will be ignored or distorted. Michael, who we met earlier, had come to believe that the world is an uncertain place where closeness inevitably leads to abandonment. In order to survive he had decided to substitute control for closeness. Any attempt at conveying warmth or affection would be viewed as manipulation. For Tony, in Chapter 2, rejection had led him to conclude that it is better not to act for fear of getting it wrong.

The challenges associated with the developmental processes outlined in Chapter 2 can be linked to particular script decisions (Bott, 1988). The original script theory outlined by Berne (1961) and his colleague Claude Steiner (1974) has subsequently been extended by Taibi Kahler (Stewart & Joines, 1987) with the proposal that the central features of an individual's life-script are repeatedly played out over a short time period. These are indicated not only by words but also through voice tone, gesture, posture and facial expression (i.e. analogically, see Chapter 3). These behavioural sequences enacted in the therapy room can be viewed as the royal road to process in that they open the way to useful speculation about the origins and persistence of the issues the client brings while suggesting ways in which these might be engaged with productively. It should be made clear that this is not a matter of interpretation but one of making thematic inferences from observable behaviours.

Lucy had come to therapy following the break-up of a long-standing relationship. Although her partner had always expressed doubts about being with her and she had suspected him of having been unfaithful on more than one occasion, his departure seems to have taken Lucy completely by surprise. Throughout their time together, Lucy had put everything she could into making her partner happy. In her first session, tears welling up in her eyes, she described herself as being devastated. She was clearly experiencing immense distress at the loss. We might conclude that she had failed to make him happy and now things have gone badly wrong. Like the protagonist in the Greek myth, Lucy lived and lives with the Sword of Damocles hanging over her head. In her case this takes the form of the feared rejection that will follow if she fails to please.

Driver behaviour

As Lucy tells her story, the content of the session, you notice the way that it is told. Her voice is high-pitched and has the tone you might associate with a little girl rather than a mature woman of 35 years. Despite her distress there is a tense smile and she nods vigorously when you speak. Her shoulders are hunched up and she leans towards, you looking up with her face turned downwards. The story is being acted out in the room. In subsequent sessions you notice that Lucy comes early and there is a sense that your arrival is eagerly awaited. By the same token she becomes anxious prior to the end of the session, concerned that she is taking up too much of your time. Alongside the observation of this behaviour, the warm glow you experience in relation to your work with Lucy confirms that she is setting out to please you. What you are experiencing is 'driver' behaviour. As we have seen, the script arises from the child's 'decision' in the face of a parent 'message'. Here the message is 'You are OK when you …', to which the child responds with the decision 'I am OK when I …'. The term 'message' might be misleading here. As the opening section of this chapter suggests, it does not refer to a particular direct exchange but to an extrapolation by the child from a constellation of experiences in early life. This will become clearer on closer inspection of Lucy's dilemma. Five typical driver behaviours are identified:

- Be perfect
- Try hard
- Be strong
- Hurry up
- Please (others)

Typically, a client showing 'be perfect' driver behaviour will over-detail in their exchanges with you with frequent parentheses to make sure their expression is accurate. This will be delivered in an even voice-tone and their posture will be rigid and still. They have been shown and told that they need to be perfect and mistakes are unacceptable. Their script will require that they cover everything before they can relax. When faced with 'try hard', there are likely to be frequent references to need to try delivered in a tense and muffled voice tone. The person will visibly strain in their chair and go round and round, never actually getting anywhere. The client who has decided to 'be strong' has come to the conclusion that they will only be OK if they hide their feelings and don't let others see how weak they feel inside. This will show itself in a closed posture and an aggressive manner. You will find yourself blamed and driven away as the client deprives her- or himself of the rewarding contact they long for. When engaging with 'hurry up' you will find yourself in the presence of breathless agitation, probably following a late arrival. For this client there is no time to stop, think and make contact. Sentences will be scrambled and words gabbled. Their gaze will continually shift with a frequent examination of their watch.

Those familiar with the notion of personality structure will recognise features of obsessive, paranoid, passive-aggressive and hysteric presentations. The significance here is that the relational themes associated with these structures are presented as observable behaviours and available to process intervention on the part of the therapist. The compulsion to 'be perfect' can be challenged by a new 'message' that 'You are good enough the way you are'. The client exhibiting 'try hard' behaviour is challenged to 'do it without a struggle'. Being strong is met by a context where it is OK to show feelings and ask for what is wanted. Agitation and a refusal to think is met with the firm containment that makes for safe contact. Of course, as we have seen, this is not a simple matter of pointing out driver behaviour and inviting the client to substitute more productive behaviours. If it were as simple as that, this book would be pointless and we would all be out of a job.

Lucy is showing 'please others' driver behaviour in enacting the script belief that 'If I don't make others happy, things will go badly wrong'. In order for her to be happy she must first make you happy too. This leads to some useful speculation. Where Tony had suffered defeat in exclusion from his parents, it could be inferred that Lucy had actually won the Oedipal battle (see Chapter 2). The psychoanalytic literature would suggest that this is equally problematic developmentally. Victory over the same-sex parent constitutes a direct threat to the relational security, which follows from an optimal response where the Oedipal challenge is met by just and firm controls. If the young child is successful in their 'seduction' they find themselves caught in a perverse triangle, where in order to retain the attention of one parent they need to continue to make them feel good while at the same time the threat to the other parent might open the way to the script decision 'to stay young and not be a threat'. A systemic view would be that the child occupies a particular position in the system where they carry the responsibility for the family's emotional climate.

In her various attempts to please you, Lucy is enacting her old role in the parental dynamic and the family system. This has also been acted out in her failed relationship. Inevitably, sooner or later Lucy will run out of the enormous energy that is required to keep things going and the sword of Damocles, which has been suspended over her head, will fall. We have seen how the vacuum of the consulting room invites an enactment of the dilemma. At this point you stand in for all the others who have to be pleased in order to keep catastrophe at bay. The least helpful thing you can do is collude with her and accept this invitation.

While we are about this we might reflect on how the notion of driver behaviour relates to the clients we have already met. Tony showed every indication of needing to 'be perfect', while Michael dealt with the world by being 'strong'. For Tony the crucial shift was to take a position of accepting being good enough, and here he was aided by a therapist who clearly demonstrated that she did not need to get things right. The work with Michael revolved around his discovery that he could be open and experience his wants and needs. However, it is unlikely that he would be in a position to do this if the significance of his protective strategy had not been acknowledged and respected by the therapist. The task Lucy is facing is to find a way of taking her power back and pleasing herself.

Repetition compulsion and game theory

In Chapter 1 it was suggested that we each have a 'compulsion' to repeat the past in the present. As we have seen, for Freud this was a matter of unconsciously returning to an unresolved developmental task in an attempt to master it. Bowlby would understand it as the way models of the world internalised in infancy are imposed on the world where, for contemporary neuroscience, this is a function of the manner in which the brain is actually built in early life. These principles will be revisited in Chapter 8 when we explore the notion of persistence in greater depth. Berne used the term 'game' to account for this phenomenon. Where the notion of 'script' accounts for the 'life plan' of an individual, game theory provides a way of understanding and working with its day-to-day expression. As such it provides a powerful tool for engaging effectively with process. A 'game' consists of a series of exchanges which seem socially plausible but have an ulterior meaning psychologically in as much as they reinforce a decision in childhood. The game ends at the point where the player experiences a familiar bad feeling or state of mind. In accounting for this apparently unproductive and self-destructive process, Berne proposes two axioms. These are what he calls 'the hunger for strokes' (i.e. the emotional experience that comes from contact with and recognition by others) and 'the hunger for structure'. The task for each of us as human beings is to structure our time while finding ways of being in human contact which give rise to feelings. As we have seen in the clients we have met, intimacy carries with it dangers. Playing a game, by contrast, takes us to a familiar 'scripty' place with its attendant bad feelings. In short, we give ourselves a 'safe' emotional experience, albeit one which reinforces a unproductive view of the world.

In order to bring this to life, ask yourself the following questions:

- What keeps happening over and over again that leaves you feeling bad?
- How does it start?
- What happens next?
- And then?
- How does it end?
- How do you feel?
- How do you think the other person feels?

Stewart and Joines (1987) propose that you also ask yourself two mystery questions:

- What is your secret message to the other person?
- What is the other person's secret message to you?

You may have surprised yourself with the ease by which you are able to identify a repeated theme or pattern in your life that carries with it a familiar state of mind. Reflecting on your 'secret message' and speculation about the other person's gives a clue to the psychological level of the exchange. Now go back to your childhood and the times when things went wrong or you were under stress. What was happening and how did you feel about it? In TA this feeling is called a 'racket feeling' – a familiar emotion which was learned and reinforced in childhood. It may seem counter-intuitive, but the purpose of the game is to construct a situation where the racket feeling can be legitimately experienced. This provides the emotional charge from contact with others for which we 'hunger' without the attendant risks of intimacy. We may be distressed, but it is distress which is very familiar.

Before proceeding, you might give yourself some time to reflect upon any themes and patterns you have identified and any connections you are able to make between these and your place in the family in which you grew up. As was suggested in Chapter 3, it is highly unlikely that your choice of profession is a matter of either chance or even a conscious decision to be helpful to others. There is every possibility that it represents an attempt to resolve a dilemma in your own family life. One scenario might be that you carried the responsibility for others in the family at an early age by virtue of a parent's physical or emotional unavailability. In adult life this might well show itself in a personal process, not unlike Michael's, of taking responsibility for others at the expense of your own needs, such as 'being strong'. In essence, the therapist–client dynamic becomes one where the therapist fails to meet their own needs, projecting them onto the client and taking care of them instead. This opens the way to an unproductive exchange in which a 'victimised' client comes to resent their 'rescuer'. A more typical presentation is closer to Lucy's. The role of therapist provides a context in which the archaic responsibility for the emotional wellbeing of the family can be re-enacted with the unsuspecting client as surrogate for the original figures. It goes without saying that setting out to 'please' your clients does not make for good therapy. Not only is little of any value likely to happen but also, as we have seen, you will find yourself increasing infuriated by your client's apparent refusal to get better. That said, all is far from lost. Having the measure of your own process opens the way to turn a liability into an asset. The ability you developed as a child in order to 'read' what was happening around you emotionally is the very quality that you need in order to work effectively with process. In short, effectively your 'training' to be a therapist started long before you applied for a course.

It is important to stress that we do not set out to play games and neither do our clients. They happen unconsciously as we act out and confirm our understanding of the world or frame of reference. Effective therapeutic intervention requires the identification and subversion of games with a view to bringing them into awareness. How this is done is a matter of modality and personal style but one thing is clear: teaching clients about their games has limited therapeutic value. Classical TA typically took place in groups where the therapist had a flip-chart to hand in order to explain to the client what game they were playing and how it connected to script and so on. There is some merit in this, but we need to keep in mind the circumstances in which the dilemma that is being repeated was first experienced. For the young infant, entirely dependent on another for survival, it is no exaggeration to suggest that this would have been a matter of survival. Further, if knowing something were not good for us were the basis for change, we would all be sticking to our New Year's resolutions instead of abandoning them on the third day of January. As was suggested in Chapter 3, second-order change comes out of a crisis which requires significant rearrangement of our taken-for-granted world. It follows that the exchange with the therapist needs to carry some of the intensity of the context and dynamics in which the original 'decision' was made. Change requires a dramatic, or at least unexpected moment within a relationship that has significance.

Discounting

The alternative to naming the client's process is to engage with it in such a way that the anticipated outcome is replaced by an unpredicted event. When this happens the world can no longer be taken for granted and a limiting frame of reference is expanded. To achieve this we need to get a sense of how the frame of reference is maintained. A helpful framework is proposed by Schiff, Mellor, Richman, Fishman, Wolz and Mombe (1975). They use the term 'discounting' to describe the process whereby the full possibilities of the world are distorted in order to conform with an infantile script decision. Here, some aspects of experience are ignored while others are exaggerated. We have seen the way in which Lucy failed to react to her doubts about her ex-partner and his infidelity. She had remained passive in the face of his significantly unacceptable behaviour and his departure had taken her by surprise. This redefinition of consensual reality shows itself in two typical therapist–client exchanges. In a tangential transaction the client diverts the therapist away from an issue which they perceive as a threat. This kind of exchange may well have shown itself at the start of the work with Lucy. If you had asked her 'What do you want from coming to see me?', her response might have been something along the lines of 'Lots of people recommended you'. The pre-occupied therapist may have let this pass, but the process is already being played out. Lucy is showing you the way in which she does not get her needs met. When asked what she wants she goes off on a tangent based on an assumption about what you might want – praise. An appropriate response from the therapist might be: 'That I am widely recommended makes me feel warm inside, but I'm no clearer about what you would like.' In process terms, no matter how unformed Lucy's identification of her needs might be, the fact that she makes a demand – any demand – is significant. Aspects of the world that are perceived to be threatening to the client's frame of reference may also be directly blocked by a redefinition of the exchange. This might go as follows:

> *Therapist:* Is there anything you would like to be different about your life?
> *Lucy:* I'm sorry, what do you mean by different?

The therapeutic task is to challenge the passivity that is an indication of discounting. In Lucy's case this shows itself as over-adaptation. While she may appear to be behaving in a socially acceptable manner, in effect she is no less passive than if she were to doing nothing at all. At an infantile level, Lucy is complying with what she believes others want instead of acting on her on account in order to meet her needs. Time and again when working with Lucy you will find yourself drawn into a 'game'. Lucy will set out to find a way of placing you on a pedestal, anticipating your every need. Between sessions she will castigate herself for her failure to make you happy. The final payoff will be a racket feeling in the form of fear of retribution combined with a sense of inauthenticity. Beneath this there will be a deep rage that no one is meeting her needs.

Effective therapy will be taking place each time Lucy's attempt to please you is countered by a refusal to be pleased. In addition, the therapist might make the proposal that she draw on both her thinking and latent anger in order to make the demands whereby she pleases herself. That said, something else needs to happen in the therapy before she is in a position to do this. Here, we might revisit the work with Michael outlined in Chapter 3. You will recall that in order to engage with Michael it was necessary to give careful attention to his need to protect himself from closeness. Lucy's needs are quite different. She needs to feel that she is loved and appreciated before she can access her thinking.

Some of these dynamics are captured with elegance and deceptive simplicity by Paul Ware (1983) and have been developed further by drawing on the work of Taibi Kahler (1975) referred to above. Ware has developed a framework which identifies six 'personality adaptations': hysteric, obsessive-compulsive, schizoid, antisocial, passive-aggressive and paranoid. In this model Lucy would be regarded as 'hysteric'. She has received 'messages' that she should not grow up, think or be important and, as we have seen, has come to the conclusion that she should please others. For each of these 'types' Ware identifies what he calls an 'open door' and a 'target door'. Most of the 'hysteric's' energy goes towards feeling, and this is the 'open' door to which therapeutic intervention should initially be directed. This opens the way to move on to the 'target door', which is thinking, in order for her to separate and grow up. It follows that connection with Lucy is best achieved by responding to her in an emotionally nurturing manner before challenging her refusal to think and take responsibility. This contrasts with Tony, whose 'obsessional' tendencies suggest that he requires recognition of his thinking before he is ready to move to feelings. For Michael, acknowledgement of his belief system is central to making contact. Where Lucy needs to feel loved and cared for in order to think, Michael needs to feel respected and to be in control in order for feeling to be a possibility.

Games therapists play – the drama triangle

As Claude Steiner reminds us (1974), Berne makes a distinction between the genuine helping, which is a feature of everyday social life, and what he termed 'rescuing': a game based on the belief that people cannot really be helped. This has particular significance for the authors and readers of this book. We have made helping a career opportunity and, as with others in the helping professions, we run the risk of engaging in unproductive and even harmful exchanges with those we set out to help.

The rescue game entails the taking of three roles: victim, rescuer and persecutor. This is also known as 'the drama triangle', shown in Figure 5.1 (Karpman, 1968). The victim takes a position that they are not OK but others are. Presenting themselves as helpless and hopeless they invite the rescuer to *try* to help them. The rescuer responds with a willingness to try to help despite the hopeless nature of the victim's predicament. They are OK precisely because the victim is not, and needs their help. Previously we have seen the problem of managing a spoiled identity in the work of Erving Goffman. Also, in a moment of honesty, we have acknowledged the seductive quality of our identity as a therapist. Systemic thinking has introduced us to the notions 'circularity and complentarity', whereby positions in a relationship become mutually reinforcing. The more the rescuer tries to help, the more the victim's hopelessness is confirmed. As the victim becomes increasingly passive and helpless, so the rescuer has to mobilise increasing amounts of energy in trying to help. At this point something has to give. This dynamic is best illustrated in the game Berne calls 'Why Don't You, Yes But'. The victim presents a problem to the rescuer who responds in what they believe to be a helpful way, only to have their attempts at helpfulness ignored or rejected. This only organises the rescuer to seek more solutions which, after indications of a passing show of interest, are again discarded by the victim. At this point the rescuer, infuriated by the victim's refusal to be helped, switches to persecutor and attacks the victim for their ingratitude. The point here is that the rescuer, in as much as they disqualify and discount the abilities of the

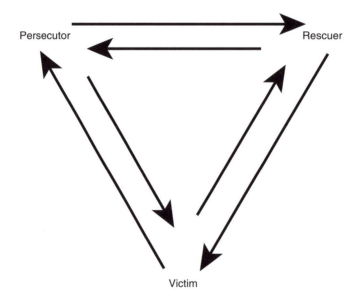

Figure 5.1 The drama triangle

person taking the victim role, harms rather than helps. By the same token the victim covertly persecutes the rescuer in retaliation for being shamed.

Those of you who have been in practice for a while will recognise the process by which your initial enthusiasm has become worn down by clients who reject your best efforts by simply refusing to get better. This has been compounded by false hope when progress has been made but no real change has taken place. You have found yourself harbouring negative and persecutory feelings and may even have shocked yourself by engaging in aggressive interventions dressed up at the time as necessary confrontation. This unfortunate situation will have come about because at some level you have failed to see the client as a complete human being who is capable of taking power over their life. In TA terminology, you will have slipped from the constructive position of 'I'm OK, you're OK' to one of 'I'm OK, you're not OK'.

To summarise, in every situation where someone needs help from another person there is the potential for a rescue game to be played out. As we have seen, the nature and intensity of the therapeutic relationship combined with the 'script' tendencies of the therapist creates a context where there is a high probability for rescuing to take place. Claude Steiner (1974) makes some helpful suggestions about how this might be avoided:

- Do not help without a contract.
- Do not believe that the client is helpless.
- Help those feeling helpless to find their power.
- Do not do more than 50 per cent of the work.
- Do not do anything that you don't really want to do.

Contracting is a formal procedure within TA but the general principle has application to all therapeutic approaches. Here, the therapist actively engages with the client in finding out explicitly what they want from therapy. The therapist only agrees to a request if it is something that can be achieved and that they are competent to provide. Equally, the therapist may make an offer but only proceeds when the client has explicitly agreed to accept it. For example, the client may say that they have come to therapy to be made happy. In fact, it is reasonable to assume that at an unspoken level this is precisely why most of our clients come to us. Clearly, in the absence of magic, the therapist faces an impossible task. Given this, an appropriate response might be along the lines of:

> This is a perfectly reasonable request since you are giving up your time and spending money, but the best I can do is think with you about your unhappiness and what you might do differently in order to have a more enjoyable life. Will that do?

The therapist then waits for an answer. If the client says 'yes', a contract has been established and the therapist has refused to take the position of doing something the client hasn't asked for, which, more to the point, would create a context where the client becomes the helpless recipient of the therapist's interventions while carrying no responsibility for the outcome, that is, one where the therapist does more than 50 per cent of the work. This dynamic is played out not only at the beginning of the work, but is visited and revisited throughout therapy. Whenever the client takes a victim role or the therapist acts as rescuer, persecution by one or the other is highly likely to follow.

Experience suggests that the avoidance of rescuing is open to misunderstanding. It is not unusual to find trainees, so terrified of being accused of being 'rescuers' that they have forgotten what it means to be kind. The people who come to see us are in distress and vulnerable. We should never forget that warmth and human kindness are appropriate responses to this. The point is that this should not be delivered from a one-up position. At the same time, avoiding being one-up is not an excuse for poor appearance, bad time-keeping and general incompetence. On the contrary, an 'I'm OK, you're OK' position requires respectful and effective practice.

6   An Inability to Relate

> **"How can I get love and still be self-sufficient?"**

Riddled with flu, a therapist rings each of her clients to announce that she would unfortunately need to cancel the following day's sessions. Hearing her audibly unwell, her clients, some sounding more sincere than others, offer polite wishes for recovery and make understanding noises about the absence. Making her final call, she remembers it is Rebecca and braces herself. 'Oh, I see,' Rebecca says coldly, 'this is possibly the worst time for you to cancel as I have my audition on Friday.' Awkward goodbyes are said and as the therapist lowers the phone, she feels a mixture of anxiety, guilt and anger. She begins to question how unwell she really is: could she drag herself in tomorrow? Upon reflection, and with a thermometer reading of 39.2, she crawls back to bed and wisely stays there.

The reader will have encountered Rebecca before, if not in their consulting room then certainly at work or at home. Rebecca is not easy to like and is experienced by her therapist (and others, we suspect) as arrogant, self-absorbed and controlling. She speaks with scathing disdain of others' aesthetic flaws and is aggressively competitive in her failing career as a commercials model. What is not immediately apparent, however, is that Rebecca has begun suffering from panic attacks when on her own in her flat at night and this has led her to seek the help of her GP. He suggested psychotherapy as all other medical checks have proved unfruitful.

Rebecca was an educated, glamorous woman in her early 30s and the therapist was struck by the impoverished world that she inhabited. Her 'friendships' took the form of superficial, cocaine-fuelled social encounters and, by way of intimacy, Rebecca entertained a series of men but had failed to make a lasting connection with any of them. She did not seem dissatisfied with this state of affairs: life was pretty good actually, if only the 'damn panic-attacks would just go away'. She entered therapy with a request that the therapist do just that: make the panic attacks go away. She had no sense of curiosity about why these were happening to her and certainly did not feel that she could have any role in making these disappear. Eliciting information regarding her early life was not easy as Rebecca always had her latest 'triumph' to report during her therapy sessions and expressed a deep irritation when the therapist showed an interest in her past. Her panic attacks were a thing of the present, she said, and the past is over and done with in any case.

Initially, Rebecca's therapist found the sessions to be full of content and much information regarding her present life was seemingly offered. Rebecca did not find it difficult to fill up the sessions. However, as time wore on the therapist became aware of a growing feeling of dread, coupled with a disturbing sense of impotence, at forthcoming sessions. Even the most innocuous reflective interventions seem to hang in the air between them. The therapist's use of language felt clumsy and ill-timed. A growing hostility began to brood in the room. The therapist compensated for her sense of inadequacy by attempting to sharpen her empathic antenna as a way of addressing her failure to set up a constructive therapeutic alliance.

It often comes as something of a surprise to colleagues early in their training when a client, such as Michael in Chapter 3, is encountered who behaves as if other people's warmth and concern (let alone love) are toxic substances. As Rebecca recounted her life's stories and indifferently answered probing questions about her past, she revealed a series of missed opportunities for intimacy and creativity. Though not directly communicated, the therapist discerned a disappointment in her failure to really succeed as a model – when starting out her ambitions had been high – and a growing resentment that her not insubstantial intellect had not been put to professional use. Whenever there had been an opportunity for a lasting connection with a partner, Rebecca had turned away and chosen to chase idealised, beautiful others instead. Expressions of love towards her were always viewed with suspicion, as obvious signs of the other's weakness and neediness.

Other people's mortal flaws were generally reported through biting disgust and the men who fell in love with her were discarded as dead-weights. Her desire for them vanished overnight once she saw their 'weak and clingy' real selves. From a distance, she admired the 'beautiful people' from the fashion world and identified with what she perceived to be their happiness and fulfilment. Her personal life took on a very transient feel therefore, as when their perfection was punctured through familiarity, she moved on to the next. There was no genuine sense that a real other might have something to offer her. As the reader can no doubt imagine, this made therapy a very tricky proposition.

Conversely, Rebecca displayed a high sensitivity to criticism and a tendency to see such where none was intended. Her hunger for revenge was voracious. Once, when a girlfriend beat her to a role in an audition, she wrote to her son informing him that his mother had been having an affair for some time. This was reported in therapy with a strong sense of justice having been done and with no obvious regret, let alone shame. This ruthlessness and highly developed sadistic streak left her therapist feeling icy cold. Meanwhile, Rebecca's panic attacks flared up whenever she was alone in her flat, and she protected herself against these by staying out late and self-medicating with drugs and alcohol. This was having a detrimental effect on her work as her appearance was the tool of her trade and she was beginning to elicit remarks about her distressed skin and increasingly sunken eyes.

Once again, there are a number of theoretical lenses through which we could begin to look at Rebecca's deeply troubled life. Her inability to love or be loved made for a depleted internal world and, as compensation, she turned to idealised notions of 'perfection' which she oscillated between locating in herself or in fantasy others. When this exhausting charade invariably collapsed, denigration followed. When she located this disgust in others, the problem was easily solved as she discarded them from her life. When this collapse took place in relation to her very fragile self-image, however, this placed her in grave danger as the level of self-disgust and self-loathing she experienced had the potential to threaten her very psychic existence. The Kleinians amongst you will not have failed to see evidence of splitting here, and this will lead you to conclude that she had failed to reach the depressive position. Those of a person-centred disposition will be wondering about the messages given to Rebecca in infancy about what it meant to be 'good enough'. Those given to thinking in terms of TA might well consider the implications of Kahler's 'be perfect' driver (see Chapter 5) where the individual feels a compulsion to be wonderful and correct in every way and expects others to do the same.

Rebecca's need to be admired and experience herself as perfect pointed to a strong narcissistic streak. Here, we might also usefully turn to psychoanalytic writings to make sense of the symbolic prison that Rebecca had created for herself, and the not inconsiderable challenge faced by her therapist in attempting to reach her client through a concrete wall. The literature suggests that the type of client who might attract the label 'narcissistic' often represents the greatest challenge to experienced and novice therapists alike. In equal measure, however, is the level of distress and despair experienced by individuals finding themselves in Rebecca's type of 'secure prison'.

Narcissism

Let us then turn our attention to ways of understanding narcissism. First, it is important to remind ourselves that there is an obvious and inherent danger in the process of labelling. It has been our experience that when discussing concepts such as narcissism with training groups, there is a tendency for the discussion in the group to refer to 'The Narcissist' as if these monstrous people are totally *other* to the rest of us. As Neville Symington (1993) reminds us, locating all that is bad in the other is a fundamental characteristic and function of narcissism. This is an obvious pitfall for therapists and training groups alike. There is nothing like working with very unlikeable and aggressive clients to mobilise narcissistic tendencies in therapists. We would argue that narcissistic qualities are present in all of us, therapist and client alike, and that the concept needs to be considered as a spectrum of severity.

Much is often said, and joked about, in therapeutic circles regarding the benefits of *positive* or *healthy* narcissism. By this we tend to mean having a good dose of self-esteem capable of experiencing both pride and the quick recovery from mild blows to one's ego. What we know about Rebecca, and others with whom the reader will be familiar, is that even the mildest of criticisms are experienced as a psychological catastrophe. These have the power to elicit unprecedented expressions of rage and self-loathing.

A fascinating polemic has existed within the psychoanalytic literature regarding the origins of narcissistic traits. These have been described as: a notable absence of empathy towards others; ruthlessness; an insatiable need to be admired; a grandiose and omnipotent personality which often collapses into intense feelings of worthlessness and inferiority; a tendency towards the idealisation or denigration of others; and an unusual degree of self-referencing and self-centredness. A comprehensive account of the literature is outside the scope of this chapter; however, no discussion would be complete without the mention of three influential thinkers on the subject: Sigmund Freud, Otto Kernberg and Heinz Kohut.

What follows is an introductory exposition of the central themes found in the literature on narcissism and of the differences articulated by these three psychoanalytic thinkers. Readers who have a particular interest in the subject are encouraged to access the primary texts. Students of counselling and psychotherapy often request accessible summaries of the central themes concerning narcissism and what follows attempts to provide just that. It may help the reader unfamiliar with this material to bear in mind the following distinctions between the three writers: for Freud, narcissism found in adulthood can be understood as being largely 'defensive' in the sense that it represents an attempt by the individual to protect oneself from suffering. Kernberg, by contrast, takes the view that narcissism is to be understood as being largely 'destructive' in that the individual is motivated to attack *the other* out of feelings of envy and frustration. Finally, a Kohutian account does not emphasise either its defensive or destructive elements, but represents an arrested development by the individual on the way to maturity. Let's now consider each in further detail.

Freud's interest and writings regarding narcissism span a 30-year period and important revisions to his original thinking occurred in line with his secondary structural model of the mind. In essence, Freud came to distinguish between what he called *primary* and *secondary* narcissism, seeing the former as an appropriate developmental stage and the latter as a pathological regression sometimes present in neurosis. The Freudian infant is one which is born without a sense of distinction between himself and the world around him. Primary narcissism refers to a stage of normal infant development where the infant experiences himself and his world as one and does not make any distinction between self and other. The actions of *the other* are therefore experienced as being under the infant's omnipotent control. This illusory state, however, is destined for disappointment as increased cognitive awareness and inevitable frustrations confront the infant with their separation from, and consequent need of, others. Secondary narcissism, by contrast, relates to a regressive move on the part of the individual to withdrawing libidinal investment (which might helpfully be thought of as love) from 'objects' in the external world and directing such love towards the self. For those unfamiliar with psychoanalytic terminology, 'objects' refer to important others in an individual's life and their corresponding mental representations in our internal world. What is being proposed here by Freud is a continuum which places narcissism at one end and the capacity to engage in 'object love' at the other. He states:

> A strong egoism is a protection against falling ill, but in the last resort we must begin to love in order not to fall ill, and we are bound to fall ill if, in consequence of frustration, we are unable to love. (Freud, 1914a, pp. 67–102)

Freud reminds us of the vulnerability and risk inherent in loving when he states that 'a person in love is humble'. The ability to love an *other*, therefore, is the antithesis of narcissism. To love is to risk and to renounce the love affair that, as babies, we had with ourselves.

A crucial statement is buried in the quote borrowed above. Freud offers that one might be unable to love *in consequence of frustration*. The question then arises: What 'frustration' could have such powerful and catastrophic effect? Imagine the infant who cannot 'find' a mother – who when confronted with the mother sees an empty void, or worse, a hostile and attacking other who fails to provide what the infant needs. In order to believe in goodness, to preserve the notion that the world is a safe-enough place, the infant will, as a last resort, turn to loving itself and to locating all that is good, and by implication denying all that is bad, within the confines of that self. *Secondary narcissism* relates to the defensive position developed by the individual who, in the face of this type of Freudian 'frustration', takes himself as his own love object in a desperate attempt to keep the notion of 'good' alive in his world. This constellates around the notion of the *ego ideal* which Freud suggests forms the cornerstone of the narcissistic conflict. In the consulting room, and elsewhere for that matter, this can be seen by the tendency to display inflated, grandiose, omnipotent accounts of oneself and, conversely, the compulsive denigration of others. These often lead to acts of hubris which have the effect of compounding deep-seated (often unconscious) beliefs that the person is truly unlovable. Others who can bolster up our fragile self-image of perfection need to be found, and it is not uncommon for this to translate into sexual promiscuity and substance misuse which help prop up the charade of omnipotence. Obsessions with idealised unavailable others can also be understood in this vein.

As stated earlier, Kernberg, with his Kleinian routes, saw the manifestation of narcissism as essentially *destructive* as opposed to *defensive* (Kernberg, 1970). Kernberg's account describes an infant who hates and envies the other for its power to withhold or to frustrate and upon whom they depend. This terror of dependency leads to the attempts to psychologically annihilate the other. This is substituted by fantasies of omnipotence and an inflated view of the self and its own 'specialness'. As the object has been psychically destroyed, these fantasies of idealism are often projected onto others in an attempt to resurrect the notion of an other who contains all that we need. As one client expressed, 'What I want most in the world is to believe that there is someone out there who is truly separate and truly benign.' On occasion, severely narcissistic clients will invest the therapist with this quality, particularly in the early stages. Therapists should beware as this is a considerable height to fall from. A male client became intensely preoccupied with his belief that his therapist was a wonderful mother at home who cared for her children in an idyllic, selfless manner. More commonly, however, such idealisation is reserved for the self, but the fall is equally as dramatic. Kernberg suggests that beneath such grandiosity are profound feelings of emptiness and rage at the helplessness the individual feels in the face of the other. The smallest 'slight' can have the power to provoke the person to fly into a rage or bring on the most inconsolable despair. He states: 'a hungry, enraged, empty self full of impotent anger at being frustrated and fearful of a world which seems as hateful and revengeful as the patient himself' (Kernberg, 1974).

For Kernberg, the infant seeks to destroy and obliterate the other, leading to envious and exploitative relationships in adulthood and the self-centred narratives that keep others at a distance. We all have had a friend whose phone calls we dread as we know we will be subjected to long, protracted accounts of their latest dramas and triumphs. What we notice during these exchanges is that we feel a mixture of boredom and anger as we are organised into the role of passive audience: our own recent happenings and concerns are met with silent disinterest and tangential responses. In the consulting room this translates into the therapist's interventions or interpretations being met with indifference or cutting retorts on the part of the client. One therapist, on expressing the progress which she felt had been made during the previous session to her male client, was met with the reply 'It's kind of irrelevant what you think – that's not how I saw it at all'. What we see here can be understood as an attack on the therapist's subjectivity motivated by a hatred of the other's separateness (Kernberg, 1965). Equally, the client referred to earlier who idealised his therapist's mothering could also be seen as objectifying her, as her own struggles or needs as a person could not be recognised. In the case of Rebecca we can see that once others reveal their inner world they become intolerable to her.

Working with clients experiencing this type of suffering, and suffering it certainly is, leads one to the conclusion that in the moments when a grandiose and inflated self-esteem is punctured the client eventually connects to a profound sense of hopelessness. The infant needs to have hope that good exists in the world and that love is available. If the world, for whatever reason, is not perceived to be offering this, the infant will, as a last resort, take the self as its own love object in order for hope to survive. Therapists should take heed: to insensitively deflate the unrealistic grandiosity of a severely narcissistic client can have catastrophic consequences.

Heinz Kohut, contemporaneous with Kernberg, takes issue with Freud's continuum theory. Narcissism and object love, he argues, are not at opposite ends of the spectrum. The infant's primary narcissism is by necessity frustrated as there will be inevitable failings in maternal care. The wish, even the *need*, to preserve this experience of bliss will split and develop, according to Kohut, along two particular strands: the 'grandiose self' and the 'idealized parent imago'. The grandiose self refers to the exhibitionist and omnipotent aspects of the child's personality. This is a normal developmental path to maturity and represents his attempts to relocate the lost sense of mastery over the environment, ruptured through the loss of primary narcissism, within the confines of the self. The idealised parent imago by contrast seeks to locate this perfection within the parent. In other words, the infant attempts to replace the loss of the experience of bliss and mastery by locating it within an idealised parent figure. This figure is not yet fully considered as a separate 'you' but rather is more akin to a concept of 'I–you'. In other words, the idealised parent imago is a function of the self. These two strands are seen by Kohut as necessary and important developmental achievements on the route to psychological maturation (Kohut, 1971, 1977).

The grandiose self of the personality refers both to the omnipotence often present in infants' fantasies as well as their exhibitionist needs. Infants' achievements of developmental milestones and creative outputs often come with a request for admiration. Equally, the rather ruthless behaviour typical of, and forgivable in, young infants belongs to this aspect of Kohut's conceptualisation of self. Gentle and benign intrusions from reality begin to temper the infant's inflated sense of self, and these modified remnants of the grandiose self become established as the cornerstone of our self-esteem. If this process is less than optimal, if the child receives too many traumatic blows to their confidence during this tender phase, these grandiose fantasies will be driven into repression and remain unmodified into adulthood. As we saw in Chapter 4, shame can be said to play a major role in bringing about this process of repression. In adulthood this can be seen as omnipotent, grandiose manifestations of the self which quickly turn into crushing experiences of shame once these fantasies come into contact with reality. The point here is that there is no integrated, healthy dose of self-esteem to protect the personality against criticism. The vulnerable aspects of the personality must not be seen at any cost. When Toto pulls back the curtain in *The Wizard of Oz*, he undoes the omnipotent and grandiose fantasy of the wizard and reveals a small, mortal man.

Notions of the idealised parent imago must too undergo modifications. A female client, the youngest of three siblings, reported on how her father used to joke with her as a child: 'You still think I'm a hero – the other two have already found out!' It is a grounding yet disturbing experience to discover our parental figures' limits and vulnerabilities. Providing the child's inevitable disillusionment takes place at a tolerable pace, and enough good in the parent can be retained and taken into the boundaries of the self, they will function as orientating images of who and how we would like to be or become. Kohut concludes that the modified grandiose self remains alive in the form of our ambitions, our desires and the introjected idealised parent imago becomes transformed into our ideals and goals. These two polarities, he argued, constituted what he called the 'bipolar self'. He concludes: 'Man is *led* by his ideals but *pushed* by his ambitions' (1966).

The manifestations of grandiosity and idealisation of both self and other respectively were seen by Kohut as a function of a developmental arrest (Kohut, 1968). In order to develop these ideals and ambitions, the infant needs others to support his process. Thus, the immature infant is dependent on the *psychological functions* provided by others. If what the infant sees is absence or depression in the eyes of the mother, then its own senses of vitality will come into question (Mollon, 1993). The others who provide these psychological functions can be said to be assisting the infant with his 'self-objects needs'. These functions or self-objects are experienced by the infant not as belonging to a separate other, but as a part of the self.

Unlike Kernberg, Kohut's diagnostic criteria for narcissism were primarily relational: what he observed were the types of relationships clients tended to form with their therapists. The Kohutian therapist conceptualises their function, with clients who present with this type of difficulty, as being placed in the role of 'self-objects'. It follows therefore that the therapist may find herself alternating between being idealised, as in the man who fantasised about her as the perfect mother, and being rendered the 'audience', as in the case of Rebecca.

How can these ideas help Rebecca's therapist find a way to connect with her? Through the theoretical perspectives outlined above, we could infer that Rebecca's panic attacks represented moments when her fantasies of self-sufficiency and grandiosity broke down and her terror of isolation broke through. In this sense, her panic attacks presented her with an opportunity to request the help of an other in the form of the therapist. Her youth and beauty had enabled her to sustain an image of herself laced with perfection and had afforded her protection from a crushing lack of self-esteem. The passing years were thwarting her ability to feed her narcissistic needs as younger models were now beating her to roles in auditions and she was confronted with the end of her modelling career. She needed help but was equally terrified to reach out for it. The panic attacks came to stand in for this ambivalence. They were the painful solution she had found to this internal conflict.

As aspects of Rebecca's early life came to light, a narrative of early parental indifference and abandonment became apparent. An only child, Rebecca had been born to parents who separated shortly after her birth. Her father vanished from their life, and as her mother struggled to make ends meet she sunk into depression and alcoholism, often leaving the young Rebecca in the care of friends and neighbours. At the age of six she was sent to live with her maternal grandparents, who were now in their later years and whom she experienced as cold and authoritarian. As adolescence came so did the pressure of exams, which her grandparents placed much emphasis on, and her failure to achieve good-enough results meant incurring their disappointment and accusations of ungratefulness for not repaying them with success. Rebecca disclosed a deep distrust of others and a fairly isolated adolescence punctuated largely by unsatisfying, and sometimes shameful, sexual encounters. A modelling career presented itself and allowed Rebecca a stage on which to shine, to become financially independent, and a world to which she could belong. This quenched her thirst for the admiration she had never received.

Being with Rebecca in the room was not an easy task. The sessions took the form of monologues and her therapist struggled to find a way in. Despite her unwillingness to invite or receive contributions from her therapist, sessions often ended with Rebecca's expressed frustrations that she 'was not getting anywhere' with the therapy. However, Rebecca was not the only one who felt alone in the room. Her therapist felt reduced to the role of useless observer. This might be seen as a recreation of the drama that brought Rebecca here in the first place: mis-attuned others who were neither able nor willing to help her.

A Kohutian approach to working with Rebecca would have it that a good dose of empathy and little by way of interpretation was required. Rebecca's grandiosity and inflated self-esteem needed attuned benign mirroring for her to be able to gradually receive a positive, yet realistic image of herself which she might begin to internalise. A therapist informed by Kernbeg, on the other hand, might have felt this approach to be too collusive and would have robustly interpreted her envious attacks on others and confronted her inner sense of despair.

The balance between empathy and collusion is a delicate one and one with which practitioners, novice and experienced alike often struggle. Our journey as clients is one best taken alongside someone who reminds us that we have (and certainly had) a right to be taken seriously, to be treated with respect and to have our inner worlds understood. This might be thought of as developing a healthy 'sense of entitlement' about taking up our position in the world. With some clients, developing a greater 'sense of entitlement' becomes a central theme of the work. We would argue, however, that once this is achieved further work is required. To live our lives in fulfilling ways we must not only be able to pursue our own desires but to understand and accommodate others' needs as well. There is a real danger that therapy stops when a healthy sense of entitlement has been developed by the client but before this has been explored in the context of the rights of others. In other words, collusion runs the danger of entrenching narcissism.

To return to Rebecca, it was clear that she was experiencing much distress, as evidenced by her panic attacks, but her ruthless approach towards others (including her therapist!) made reaching her problematic. The therapist often felt redundant in the work and yet Rebecca made it clear that she found breaks, as seen above, really very hard to tolerate. This form of ambivalence is not atypical of clients who present with what we might call strong 'narcissistic currents'. The pull is for the therapist to come under the client's omnipotent control. Whether we conceptualise this phenomenon as the therapist functioning as a Kohutian self-object or as Kernberg would have it, the client's hatred of 'separateness', the process in the room is that the therapist feels placed in the role of 'audience'; one of playing 'echo' to the client's 'narcissus'. Rebecca's need for admiration from her therapist was insatiable and any breaking of ranks was met by a series of silences, digressions or cutting remarks. Again, this is not a presentation solely reserved for clients, and the therapist must confront these tendencies in herself. One need only attend professional case discussions to experience first-hand the regular objectification of clients. Those readers who have engaged in infant observation will also have undoubtedly confronted this dynamic between mother and baby. Being at the receiving end of this type of objectification is an anxiety provoking experience as we begin to lose a sense of ourselves, question our competencies, and indeed have our capacity to think thwarted.

We can only wonder what the young Rebecca must have experienced as an infant in the care of a depressed and inebriated mother. It does not take too great a leap of the imagination to conclude that when she looked in her mother's eyes what was reflected to her was an empty space rather than a lively, inquisitive little girl eager to explore the world. We could conclude that in her infancy and childhood Rebecca too was allocated the role of 'audience', watching with impotence as her mother descended into alcoholism. Equally, with her grandparents she had never really felt 'seen' but rather was expected to perform in order to bolster up their own narcissistic needs to have a successful granddaughter.

The drama being enacted in the room provided her therapist with a powerful personal experience as to the nature of Rebecca's early experiences of self: fragmented, ungrounded, impotent, redundant. The therapist's ability to retain the capacity *to think* in these circumstances is of the utmost importance and much easier said than done. Supervision provides the therapist with an opportunity to find her voice and to resurrect the aspects of herself that have been killed off during the sessions. In learning to bring her 'aliveness' back into the therapy room and surviving, the therapist is enacting the therapeutic work unconsciously sought by the client.

In terms of process, the challenge here is for the therapist to graciously refuse the role of 'audience', but to do so in a way which is not overly threatening to the client. Experience tells us that the rage, often out of awareness, which is sometimes generated in the therapist through being silenced in this way, leads to a number of unhelpful responses depending on the therapist's own means of defence. The most common of these is that the therapist's latent anger begins to leak and their contributions in the sessions develop a subtle persecutory flavour. If the therapist's temperament is such that they are prone to high levels of warmth and a strong desire to be 'helpful', then this type of therapeutic encounter might initially lead to the therapist working terribly hard to reach her client by becoming increasingly warmer and more 'helpful'. In Rebecca's case, we saw how her therapist initially assumed that the lack of connection in the room was as a result of her failing empathic antenna. This, of course, was doomed to fail as, for Rebecca, this was a familiar pattern: she created a situation where people might try to reach her only to reject them and denigrate them for their neediness. Persisting in these patterns replayed her own childhood drama when, as a child, the needy aspects of herself were rejected by her mother. In these circumstances, the constant rebuffs of the therapist by the client may create a relational context in which the therapist, exhausted from working so hard, is likely to switch into a persecutory role. This would be more of the same for Rebecca as it would replicate exactly the type of attack and aggression she tended to experience from others in the outside world.

The question of therapeutic 'warmth' merits further reflection. There is no doubt that a good dose of warmth is important in the making and maintaining of a therapeutic alliance. A cold, withholding therapist is of limited appeal. That is not to say, however, that too much therapeutic warmth should not come with a health warning. As we saw in Chapter 3, to remain overly warm when a client is directing aggression, either conscious or otherwise, toward you as a therapist is to refuse to hear an important communication. Such aggression is communicative of early wounds and needs to be received. The therapist who is deaf to such communications runs the greatest risk of 'acting out' their latent anger through overly penetrating interventions. Such acting out on the part of the therapist threatens to compound the narcissistic wounds that the client has already experienced.

By contrast, the quiet, cool therapist might find him- or herself retreating even further into silence. Therapeutic silence certainly has its place, but people experiencing this type of distress require a therapist who is willing to make their presence felt. Not to do so places the therapist in the role of the perfect passive 'audience' unconsciously required by the client. This type of dynamic can unhelpfully go on for years, providing the perfect refuge for clients, like Rebecca, who are unable to tolerate psychological proximity. As for the therapist who is not really on top of her own narcissistic currents, an unhealthily competitive climate may develop in the work underpinned by strong feelings of mutual envy and rivalry. The point is that it is the therapist's responsibility to find a way to reach Rebecca, and clients who present in this way are often discounted as being unable to use therapy when, in actual fact, it is the therapist who has failed to get out of their own emotional comfort zone. The childhood story of Goldilocks comes to mind: the therapist needs to aim at being neither 'too warm' nor 'too cold' while monitoring her countertransference with care.

We now turn our attention to the notion of empathy. The person-centred reader will recognise empathy as one of Rogers' (1951) 'core conditions' of therapeutic practice, and there can be little doubt that helpful work cannot happen without it. For Kohut, empathy was the key to working with the narcissistically wounded client. How does this, however, sit with the Goldilocks principle described above? Rebecca arrived at her weekly sessions full of complaints regarding unhelpful, unkind or incompetent others who made her life difficult. These diatribes were expressed with hatred and a lack of reflexivity about her contribution to these relationships. To be empathic towards her complaints would be to collude with her refusal to see that she was, at least in part, the author of her own unhappiness. It is argued here that to do so is to rob the client of the autonomy she has over her life. Rebecca remained passive with regard to change: life was simply happening to her and she refused to see that she may have a role to play in mastering her panic attacks. The question of towards what, and where, we direct our empathic attunement is of the utmost importance. To empathise with her complaints about others risked colluding with her victim position. Empathy needed to be directed instead towards the narcissistic wounds Rebecca suffered as an infant and at her profound sense of isolation. For example, in response to her complaints about the unfairness of other people's actions, her therapist chose to empathise with how helpless and impotent Rebecca felt when she was unable to influence the course of events. It is only once she was able to connect to a profound sense of inner despair and helplessness, and have this acknowledged, that she could begin to address her own contribution to the state of her life. In process terms, by refusing to collude with her complaints but empathising with her distress the therapist was able to be neither too 'warm' or too 'cold'. This allowed her therapist to be present but in a way which did not further entrench Rebecca's resistance to looking at her contribution to the current state of affairs.

Others held so much power over Rebecca that they needed to be kept at arm's length, which in turn further compounded her sense of isolation and helplessness. This was being recreated in the room as the therapist too was being kept at a distance. Her therapist had to fight hard to remain separate, autonomous and yet present. It is a helpful guiding principle to keep our self-disclosures to a minimum and only to share the content of our minds when we feel it will be of direct therapeutic value to the client. In this type of therapeutic climate, however, there may be some merit in providing the client with a view into the therapist's inner world. We are talking here of the sharing of tolerable moments of difference. These might take the form of expressions of genuine surprise that a story ended in a particular way: 'I'm really surprised you said that, I thought you were going to say ...' as well as using the immediacy of the relationship through a timely invitation to explore what they imagine the therapist might be feeling. The point here is that in these moments the client *has* to acknowledge the therapist's psychological presence and subjectivity and has the opportunity to begin to tolerate this.

This is painstaking work and not for the fainthearted as it takes time, commitment and emotional robustness to withstand the attacks clients often aim at both the therapy and the therapist. The work, however, could not be more worthwhile as Rebecca was in desperate need of someone who would take her seriously and provide her with the fundamental respect and attunement she had never received. In time, she began to see that her panic attacks needed to be understood, not just be got rid of, and that they represented the vulnerable, lonely infant who was terrified of coping alone in the world. The work progresses, and by her therapist refusing to be silenced, Rebecca begins to show signs of tolerating the psychological proximity of others while accepting the needy aspects of herself.

7   Encountering Oppositionality

"How can I get my way
when I can't say what I
want?"

Mildred: What are you rebelling against, Johnny?
Johnny: Whaddya got?

The Wild One (1953)

Perhaps *Rebel Without A Cause*, the later film starring James Dean (1955), would have been a more apt title for Marlon Brando's *The Wild One*. Johnny, the character played by Brando, is anything but wild. Essentially, he does little other than react to the events which take place around him, bringing to them a brooding presence; more sulky than dangerous. The trophy he offers Kathie as a gift is stolen and, at that, won for second place. Asked what Johnny's gang are trying to prove, the Sheriff replies: 'Beats me. Lookin' for someone to push them around so they can get sore and show how tough they are … they usually find it some place or other.'

Oppositionality should never be confused with autonomy. For some, being opposi-tional has become a way of life and a virtue is made of the refusal to conform to the expectations of others. This shows itself in couple work with some frequency. The 'rebel without a cause' who appeared so noble and attractive in early adulthood has not only failed to make anything much of his life, but has also become a tiresome, sulky addi-tional 'child' adding to the burden of a long-suffering 'parental' partner. To do the opposite of what the other expects shows no more independence of thought and action than to be slavishly in thrall to their demands. At this point, we need to consider the notion of autonomy since it is problematic in itself. Our culturally common-sense view is that the self is a boundaried psychological entity. A certain kind of what we would view as naive therapeutic practice is geared towards helping what they would see as a hapless client shaking off the restrictions placed upon them by the demands and expectations of their original family. This is accompanied by the unspoken assumption that the relationship with the therapist is the only one that counts as they set out to be a better parent than the parent and a better partner than the partner. This in itself invites compliance or rebellion. If we take the view that the self is socially constructed and defined through relationship with others, then autonomous action is always situated in context and cannot be separated from the circularity of a complex relational dance. Autonomy is not distinct from relationships but situated within them.

In individual therapy, this dynamic is played out between therapist and client, with the therapist inducted into the role of the other who must be defeated. The therapist, engaging in the work with enthusiasm and good will, that is, 'trying hard' to help, finds herself frustrated, angry and even in some despair of her capacity to be of any use to the people who come to her for help. If you are engaged in practice it is likely that you will have had the experience of your client facing you squarely accompanied by an overwhelming sense that they have their back turned on you.

Mark arrives 15 minutes late for his first appointment: no explanation is made and no apology given. His opening statement is to the effect that he has no confidence in therapy and no expectation that the therapist will be able to help, but he is prepared to give it a try. Underneath his stand-off presentation there is a sense of desperation. He sits hunched in his chair, brow furrowed, visibly straining. At the age of 30 his life is going nowhere. He has recently lost his job following an argument with the boss and his girlfriend has left him. There follows an account of the unreasonable and duplicitous way his boss has behaved and of Mark's refusal to conform to his 'excessive demands'. We also learn that Mark's relationship with his girlfriend, the latest in a succession, has broken down. Mark tells the therapist that this time he had wanted things to last despite her 'unreasonable' complaint that he was not prepared to make a commitment to her. This is all delivered in an angry and impatient tone. Mark concludes with a challenge: 'Now you know the problem, tell me what to do. You're the expert!'

The therapist finds herself irritated. This is a client who does not want to be helped and is disrespectful of the profession to which she has dedicated herself for many years. Put yourself in her shoes for a moment. How do you make sense of what is happening, and what would you be inclined to say or do at this point? In doing this you will realise that the therapist is in a bind. An immediate inclination might be to lay down the law. The therapeutic frame is sacred and there has been a clear violation of structure with the late arrival. This needs to be addressed. It might be tempting to offer an insightful interpretation, which would show how sharp the therapist is, convincing Mark that he is not wasting his time. Equally, the experience of sitting in the room with this difficult and ungrateful client could prove so dispiriting that the therapist might consider referring him on to another practitioner; ideally one of whom they are not overly fond. He could give them a hard time instead. Even at this early stage the story told and manner in which it is presented opens the way to some speculation, which would suggest that neither of these options are desirable. To take up the first would be to present Mark with an attempt to control him, inviting opposition. The second would confirm that the therapist is another duplicitous authority figure with something to prove at Mark's expense. Most disastrously, referring on would leave him once more sacked and abandoned, that is, the very thing that brought him to therapy in the first place. It is entirely unreasonable to expect commitment from a client who comes to therapy presenting a problem with holding on to a job and maintaining a lasting relationship. Equally, to do nothing is to collude with Mark's unacceptable and self-defeating behaviour. In order for the therapist to be of any use and make a difference there needs to be another way.

To find this we might revisit a number of the ideas encountered in earlier chapters and draw on some others. Models of child development and script theory are helpful in speculating upon Mark's childhood dilemma and the 'decisions' that he arrived at to find a way through. Repetition compulsion and game theory provide a way of making sense of the apparently perverse and self-defeating way in which he engages with people. An understanding of the process enacted by therapist and client can be informed by communication theory, transference and driver behaviour. These ways of thinking open the way to a more productive response to Mark's perfectly understandable attempt to make the therapeutic exchange conform to his frame of reference – his insistence on persistence. At this point, we might add two other approaches which have a particularly useful part to play here. You have already encountered transactional analysis (TA) in Chapter 5 with our account of the work with Lucy. Here, we return to this model but with particular attention to ego-states and transactions. The analysis of transactions or, to put it more accurately in this case, the 'management of transactions' offers an effective way out of the bind outlined above. Finally, we return to systems thinking and the ideas first encountered in Chapter 1 drawing on narrative therapy.

Child development, scripts and games

As we saw in Chapter 4, Margaret Mahler provides a useful account of the psychological birth of the human infant which follows physical disencapsulation. Here, the mother and young infant engage in a process of differentiation moving towards physical disengagement and psychological separation. Mark's story and presentation suggest that there has been some mismanagement at the point where he made his initial bid for separation. Capable of independent locomotion, the toddler turns his or her back on the mother and seeks to engage with a wider world. This escape from close connection carries with it a sense of elation but is also fraught with risks requiring external protection and control. Anger and tantrums are an understandable response on the part of the young infant in the face of having their love affair with the world thwarted. At the same time cognitive development makes for faster and flexible thinking and, though still unable to perform abstractions and generalisations, there is an increasing capacity to shift attention from the self to the other. This makes for the beginning of the kind of internal dynamics accounted for in symbolic interactionism (see Chapter 1) as a conversation between the 'I' and the 'Me'. Mahler sees this stage as opening the way to a 'rapprochement crisis' as the infant becomes aware of the 'distance' from the mother.

Optimally, this leads to a return to close contact, but not in the form of the undifferentiated engulfment of early life. In effect, the infant has fought his or her way to separation and is on the way to becoming a differentiated individual capable of relationship without loss of independence. These ideas will be very familiar to many practitioners and central to the thinking of those who adopt a psychoanalytic approach. All readers will be able to draw on their experience of being around children. Any visit to a busy supermarket will provide a vivid illustration of this process in action as the exasperated parent wrestles with the iron will of the determined and embarrassingly noisy toddler who has a shopping list of his or her own and is eager to get to the sweets which festoon the checkout counter. Colloquially, you may know this stage of development as the 'terrible twos'.

The new ability to control bowel movement accounts for Freud's use of the term 'anal' in relation to the dynamics associated with toilet training at this stage. This provides a metaphor for other battles for control. Each developmental task carries with it a tendency towards progression and regression. Erikson (1965) sees the tension at this stage of development as one between the move towards autonomy versus the experience of shame and doubt. The optimal response on the part of the parent to this demanding time is to remain quietly encouraging while providing clearly defined limits within which the infant can safely experience his or her growing powers. This is a particularly testing time for parent and child alike.

As we saw in Chapter 5, script theory provides an account of the mechanism by which early childhood experience is carried forward into adult life. The verbal and non-verbal messages the child receives give rise to decisions which put survival before the expression and satisfaction of needs. The person-centred among you will recognise this as the process by which the 'self-concept' is formed in response to 'conditions of worth'. The frame of reference that emerges forms the basis for the manner in which the individual shapes their phenomenal world. Those of a psychodynamic disposition will account for the same phenomena by reference to transference and repetition compulsion.

At this stage it is worth repeating that we are not proposing a causal or behavioural approach where the individual is shaped by circumstances with the methodological implication that when problems arise they can be reshaped by the therapist. This belongs to a very different paradigm or set of ideas. Philosophically, the view is taken that we actively engage with and construct our world in conversation with others. Methodologically, therapeutic intervention is directed toward creating a context where the problematic aspects of this are exposed and open to reconstruction on the part of the client. In this instance we infer that the theme of dependence, independence and interdependence, which is a feature of all human life and activity, has presented a particular challenge for Mark. This leads to speculation about the way in which these themes first emerged in early life, how they were managed and the 'decisions' Mark arrived at in reaction to this. His account of the issues that brought him to therapy and the exchanges in the room suggest that he has confused action and effectiveness with resistance and rebellion. It would appear that it had been unsafe for him to say directly what he wanted but he discovered that he could hold on to a degree of autonomy by acts of refusal.

In the consulting room, driver behaviour and game theory help us to account for the drama being enacted. In this instance, we might think about the 'try hard' mode of behaviour. There is a lot of energy going into Mark's exchange with the therapist but nothing productive seems to be happening. Metaphorically, he strains on the potty but no stool is produced. Where Lucy, in Chapter 5, set out to please and tended to over-adapt to the therapist, Mark's passivity shows itself in a stubborn and resentful doing nothing. If we return to game theory and the drama triangle, we can see that Mark takes a victim position. As the therapy progresses, the therapist finds herself positioned to give advice, only to have it ignored or complained about as useless. You have already encountered the victim–rescuer dynamic in Chapter 5. With Mark there is a particular twist to this. While his presentation at a social level is as a victim, psychologically he persecutes, victimising his rescuer – the therapist. Berne outlines a number of 'games' which feature a victim-to-persecutor switch. We have already encountered the classic example: 'Why don't you, yes but'. You will recall that the victim starts with a request for help while rejecting or fending off all suggestions on the part of the rescuer. The 'switch' comes when the rescuer runs out of ideas and is rejected, revealing the hidden persecutor. 'Do me something (and I'll show you that it doesn't work)' accounts for a similar process. Here, the victim manipulates the rescuer into acting for him while remaining passive. The 'switch and payoff' come in reporting that the rescuer has given bad advice accompanied by the complaint 'See what you made me do'. Another variation is a particular version of 'kick me'. This is a dynamic whereby the victim invites punishment from a persecutor, leading to the familiar payoff of hurt. In this instance the invitation to 'kick' results in a stubbed toe. If the therapist were to take an authoritarian line in response to any acting out on Mark's part, it is highly likely that she would find herself wrong-footed.

As the therapy progresses, we learn that Mark's mother had been on her way to having some success as an actress when she had married. Surprisingly (or perhaps understandably if we were to focus on her own scripting), she had married an older conventional man who brought with him the expectation that she would give up her profession, exchanging the bright lights for a dull suburban life. Mark, an only child, found himself in a limited and limiting environment, where the excitements of his time all seemed to be happening elsewhere. Sent to a traditional grammar school, he managed to fail consistently in all subjects, leaving with few qualifications. Script theory would have it that the basic plot to the life-story written in infancy is given more detail in childhood and largely completed by the age of seven years, with some revision in adolescence. We might speculate that Mark was well on the way to living out a script which prevented him from engaging effectively with the world. He has substituted oppositionality for autonomy.

Ego-states and transactions

An understanding of ego-states and transactions can provide helpful guidelines for side-stepping the bind in which the therapist finds herself by introducing the unpredictable in a constructive way. The notion of ego-state is likely to be familiar to many readers.

That said, some accounts of TA lead to misunderstanding and the trivialisation of a subtle and, for our purposes, very useful set of ideas. A simplistic version would have it that we all have Parent, Adult and Child parts to our personality, which contain respectively: beliefs, thinking and feeling. In a similar way, those with knowledge of psychoanalytic theory may have come to the view that ego-states are merely a reductionist popularisation of Freud's original division between super-ego, ego and id. This requires some clarification, and we hope the reader will bear with a brief digression into something of a lost history. The original observation that an individual can display different ways of being does indeed belong to Freud and is present in his account of the work with Anna O in *Studies in Hysteria* (Freud & Breuer, 1895). Federn, a follower of Freud who emigrated to the USA, first coined the term 'ego-state' (Erskine, 2003). Significantly, he added to Freud's theoretical construct the experience of a state of feeling on the part of the patient. Eric Berne, who studied under Federn at Yale, extended this to include behaviour. Alongside this, Berne was profoundly influenced by Fairbairn (1952), a member of the British Object Relations School (Clarkson, 1992). Fairbairn's account of what he called 'endo-psychic structure' proposed distinct aspects of the ego: the 'central ego', the 'libidinal ego' and the 'internal saboteur'.

Thus, Berne defines an ego-state as 'a consistent pattern of feeling and experience directly related to a corresponding pattern of behaviour (1966, p. 364). The inclusion of observable behaviours in the definition of ego-states has particular significance for practice in that it opens the way for direct intervention with an externalised internal world, that is, working with process. Berne postulated the presence of what he called 'psychic organs'. The 'Archaeopsyche' is the aspect of the personality which represents the early mind and previous developmental periods; the 'Neopsyche' holds current states of mind; and the 'Extereopsyche' accounts for those aspects of the mind directly internalised or introjected from external sources. In the interests of accessibility, Berne referred to these colloquially as 'Child', 'Adult' and 'Parent' (see Figure 7.1).

When in our Parent ego-state we re-enact the feelings and thoughts of actual parent figures – the things that were actually said and done by the adults who influenced us as children. To be in Child ego-state is not merely a matter of being child-like but involves reproducing the behaviours arising from dilemmas and experiences faced in early life and actually re-experiencing the associated feelings. The Adult ego-state is concerned with the feelings, behaviours and attitudes that are a reflection of current reality.

By the time Mark entered the consulting room he was well on the way to re-enacting an archaic drama. His manner of engagement with the therapist, that is, his transferential invitation, can be understood as an outward manifestation of an intra-psychic conflict between his developmental need for autonomy and the parent figures who thwarted it. In this way, the therapist becomes for Mark a projective surrogate for the internalised parent(s) and an old battle is repeated. To quote Berne (1961), what we have here is:

> the relics of the infant who once actually existed in a struggle with the parents who once actually existed [this] reduplicates the actual childhood fights for survival between real people. (p. 66)

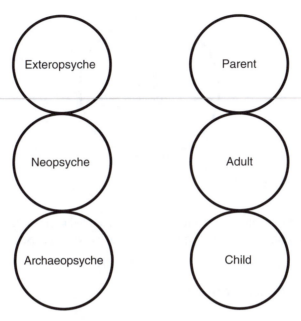

Figure 7.1 Psychic organs (after Berne, 1966)

Our grasp of this dynamic is enriched if we introduce second-order structural analysis, lost in popularised accounts of ego-states. The development of the Parent ego-state is not simply a matter of internalising rules for living. It is made up of the Parent, Adult and Child of the parents and other significant adult figures. At the risk of simplification but in the interests of clarity, Mark's parents told him he must 'try hard', an overt message from their own Parent. The Adult in the parent would have an explanation for this along the lines that 'life is a struggle'. However, his mother's Child may well have found Mark moving on in life intolerable in the light of her own lost future and the limitations imposed on her. It might be inferred that he received a covert message from his mother's Child: that he should not succeed. You will find this in the literature referred to as 'counterscript'. These are overt messages the child receives from their parents' Parent ego-state. The covert messages which originate in the parents' Child ego-state are called 'injunctions' (see Figure 7.2).

With this, Mark's father's conventional and controlling way of dealing with the world would have served to compound his dilemma. We could take the view that it is to Mark's credit that he found a way of holding out in these unpromising circumstances, but this has come at a price. As we have seen with the other clients presented in this book, his solution has now become a problem.

The process by which Mark acts out his internal world shows itself in sullen, stubborn and provocative behaviour. The desire for contact we all share is frustrated as others find themselves pushed away by his arrogant and competitive presentation or undermined by his sullen withdrawal. In all sorts of ways Mark never quite 'gets there'. This shows

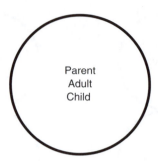

Figure 7.2   Parent ego-state

itself minute by minute in the consulting room in extended silences, repeating questions rather than answering them and frequent digressions and tangents.

Therapeutic transactions

The therapist was faced with a number of potential pitfalls. In the terminology of this approach she was invited to engage in unproductive games which would confirm Mark in his script decisions. To accept this invitation would be to take on the role of yet another parent figure to be undermined and defeated. Ego-state analysis and the management of transactions help in subverting this invitation, ensuring a more productive outcome. Mark's transactions tend to come predominantly from Child directed towards Parent, inviting a complementary response (see Figure 7.3) from the therapist, that is, Parent to Child. It is precisely this dynamic that needs to be disrupted. In excluding his Parent and Adult, Mark imposes a past dynamic on a current event. He refuses to take responsibility for himself and others while discounting current reality.

Mark comes with the expectation that others will control him and make restrictive demands. At this point the therapist has a very effective tool at her disposal – she can simply refuse to be parental. The boss, exasperated by Mark's provocation, and the girl-friend, positioned to be demanding, both confirmed Mark's expectations. Experiences in school where the classroom is often less a place of learning than a battleground where control issues are fought out, served to reinforce further Mark's view of the word. This extends back to the early scenes in infancy, reinforced by the limitations of Mark's family life. In the face of this the therapist steadfastly refuses to bring her Parent ego-state to the encounter. This is not to suggest for one moment that therapy should take place without the therapist taking responsibility. What is proposed is the acting out of a pragmatic or strategic crossing of transactions where the therapist's Parent 'stands back' and is consciously excluded from direct involvement. This has the effect of unbalancing Mark's world-taken-for-granted.

To return to the initial encounter: the irritation the therapist experiences is useful information. That said, an event is not a process, and at the beginning of the work it

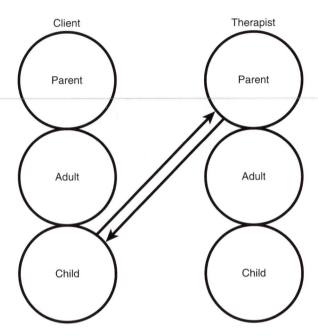

Figure 7.3 Therapeutic transactions

would not be helpful to do much more than respond with calm good humour to the perceived provocation – simply declining the invitation graciously. Given Mark's professed ambivalence, there is something to be said for showing some reluctance to engage in therapy. The less confident or experienced therapist might be inclined to convince him that therapy could be useful. A more considered response would be to suggest that Mark go away, reflect on the session, and think about whether therapy was right for him and even then if he thought the therapist was going to be of any use. You have already encountered this kind of exchange in the discussion of strategic interventions.

You may recall the way in which the therapist 'managed' Mark's sullen silences (Chapter 3) by welcoming them as a break from the demands of other clients. Here, in effect, the therapist responds to oppositionality by inviting more of it. If we bring an analysis of transactions to this, Mark's Child to Parent provocation is met at a social level by an Adult to Adult response from the therapist. However, that is not the whole story. There is another dimension to this in the form of an ulterior or non-explicit connection Child to Child (see Figure 7.4). Technically, the exchange is between the Adult in the Adult and the Child in the Adult of the therapist. For ease of understanding this second-order, structural analysis can be understood functionally as an exchange between the client's Rebellious Adapted Child directed to the therapist's Controlling Parent and responded to in Adult and Free Child. Readers who are unconcerned by these distinctions will experience no harm in putting them aside.

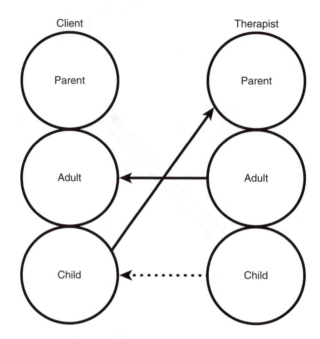

Figure 7.4 Analysis of transactions

Mark's expectations are undermined by the therapist. In being playful, she refuses to play the 'game'. So far so good, but Mark is late again for the next session. The therapist has a genuine responsibility to confront this but in doing so she risks opening the way to more of the same, particularly if this is presented in a pompous manner with a sense of knowing best. Instead, as Mark slouches into the consulting room she makes the passing remark that it is a shame that he has missed time that is rightly his but at least she has had a break between sessions since she tends to find the turn-around between clients a bit tight. Once again, an invitation to be parental has been subverted. This has been couched in terms of the therapist's Child need for a break. In process terms, the therapist's Child-focused response creates a context in which the client is placed in a position where he, albeit unwittingly, is meeting her needs. The intention here is to disrupt a negative symbiosis. As the therapy progresses, client and therapist are increasingly able to be openly playful:

> *Therapist:* I just caught myself about to make a helpful suggestion.
> *Mark:* That could be fatal.

There is a growing sense of them getting alongside one another and sharing the irony of coming for help but refusing it.

At this point you may have registered an objection. Therapy is a serious business involving vulnerable people and someone needs to be minding the shop. This becomes

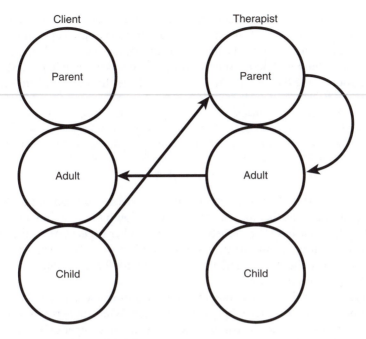

Figure 7.5   Parent-informed-Adult response

an issue as it emerges that Mark is drinking heavily. There is no place for a playful response in the face of self-destructive behaviour. Clearly, a Child-to-Child exchange is inappropriate here. At the same time, being parental would be counterproductive and likely to lead to further escalation. There is another option open here which could be understood as 'Parent informed Adult'. This would be something along the lines of the following:

> *Therapist:*   This sounds very serious. If I were in a position to tell you what to do, I'd say you need to do something about this, but there's not much I can do apart from say that since I would only be making matters worse.

Here, Mark's tendency to invite parental control in order to resist it is managed by the therapist drawing on her Parent but responding from Adult (see Figure 7.5).

Equally, we could imagine that a client presenting with similar themes to Mark might continue to show their ambivalence by poor time-keeping and sporadic attendance. If this were to become extreme it would need to be addressed. Here the therapist might intervene as follows:

> *Therapist:*   My training tells me I should be careful about structure but I am in no position to lay down the law. I'm in a bit of a fix – any ideas?

This type of transaction can be particularly helpful when working with the kind of oppo-sitionality presented by Mark. It might be thought of as taking a 'supervision' from the client. Imagine that things have got a bit stuck with Mark. They are at the point where he needs the kind of push and permission to succeed that was missing in his early life. This is a critical point in the therapy. The therapist introduces the following into the session:

> *Therapist:* I'm a bit stuck thinking that the time has come for you to move on and that there is more I should be doing. When this happens I talk to my supervisor and he usually makes a helpful suggestion or tells me where I'm going wrong. But you're the expert on Mark. How about I take a supervision from you: Am I going wrong? Is there more I should be doing?

Mark's response to this is less important than the process it sets up in the therapeutic relationship. In effect, the therapist has aligned herself with Mark in the Child-to-Parent dynamic by which she has characterised her role with her supervisor. At the same time Mark has been positioned into the Parent position of knowing best. This opens the way to a shared responsibility for finding a way forward with the intention of side-stepping Mark's habitual oppositionality.

At this point we need to re-state that the case illustration and associated interventions should not be confused with technique-driven therapy. While there is a limited place for methodology, this should not be confused with the mindless repetition of rituals and a 'one size fits all' approach to practice. If anything, we are proposing the opposite. Our view is that, subject to guiding ethical principles, the therapeutic encounter should be creative and idiosyncratic. The challenge is for you to give yourself permission to be free of the constraints imposed by the orthodoxy of your modality. Thinking about ego-states opens the way to side-stepping the repeated complementary Child-to-Parent transac-tions which characterise much of the therapeutic dynamic. If these are left uninterrupted, little that is productive will happen as old adaptations are played out with the therapist as a stand-in. Nevertheless, it would be irresponsible or misleading if you were to take away the view that the Parent ego-state should be banished from the consulting room. What is problematic for one client is indicated with another. What can loosely be termed Mark's 'passive-aggressive presentation' requires a particular kind of response. A more vulnerable client might need a protective parental response, with the therapist accepting or even inviting a degree of dependency.

The parent interview and externalising the internal family

While we are cautious about the use of technique in therapy, in this instance there is a place to consider an intervention originally developed within TA (McNeel, 1976). This is called 'the parent interview'. The therapist engages directly with externalised parental introjects with the intention of helping the client discover how his or her wants and behaviours were threatening to parent figures. This is based on the assumption that when the client was growing up, the parents were dealing with their own challenges and problems. Recognition of this opens the way to understanding and forgiveness on the part of the client while at the same time engendering cognitive restructuring. Psychodynamically, it puts the transference back where it belongs in a re-enactment of the original family dynamic. Systemically, it functions as a means of introducing information about the system into itself, the basis for second-order change (see Chapter 3). Humanistically, the client comes to recognise that parent figures were separate entities, operating from within their own frame of reference. There is a caveat here in that what is, in effect, an invitation to temporary fragmentation is inappropriate when working with clients who are vulnerable and at the risk of experiencing psychotic symptoms. For the same reason, the therapist should check whether the original parent experienced mental illness.

Those of you who are familiar with the gestalt intervention where aspects of the psyche are externalised with the client moving between chairs, will have already come across this kind of active intervention. The danger in simply re-enacting an intra-psychic conflict is that it might be reinforced rather than resolved. Here, the therapist engages directly with the parent projection by conducting an interview and even engaging in therapy with the internalised parent figure. In this instance, Mark is invited to 'be' his mother. She is then asked her name and so on and invited to talk about her experience of parenting, and specifically her emotional response to Mark's wish to engage in a more productive way of dealing with the world. Something striking about this way of working is how much we 'know' about our parents' experiences and internal worlds without knowing that we know. In taking the part of his mother, Mark comes to realise that she did not act out of malice but in response to a perceived threat against which she needed to defend herself. In present-day reality Mark comes to see his mother and father as separate from him, with their own challenges. Some familiarity with Mark's dilemma leads the therapist to ask of him as mother what the threat would be to her if Mark were to get what he wanted. At this point, as her disappointment and envy are exposed, Mark is in a position to begin to take responsibility for himself and to give up waiting for his mother to change. He declares: 'I don't have to hold myself back in order to protect you!'

There is something seductive in this kind of cathartic work and we would not like to give the impression that a dramatic event is enough in itself. Much of what is of value in the therapeutic encounter would look to the outside observer as nothing other than a prolonged and even rather dull conversation. You may actually find this type of approach uncongenial. If this is the case, there is still a value in the stark recognition of the way in which the internal impasse is enacted in the consulting room with the projection of a 'real' parent figure on to the therapist. This has the potential to inform and bring energy to working with transference.

At this point we could take the view that whatever they call themselves all therapists are really family therapists, even if they do not work with families. A number of systemic thinkers have proposed ways in which to work systemically with individuals (Allen, 1988; Bott, 1994; Jenkins & Asen, 1992). Equally, psychological approaches already address family dynamics, even if this is only implicit and under-theorised. As we have seen, the internalised family of origin is acted out in the present with partners and therapists as surrogates. One-to-one therapy by its nature tends to focus on pairings, most often on the infant–mother dyad. The crucial difference between working psycho-analytically and intervention with families is that, while psychoanalysis concerns itself with externalising an internal world, family therapy is directed towards the way in which the external world is being internalised (Dare, 1981). The recognition of this opens the way to 'bringing' other family members into the room. Those inclined to be active might surround themselves with chairs, where the more restrained amongst you might inter-vene with a question along the lines of: 'If X were here, what might he say?'

A client, Isabel, with something of a similar presentation to Mark, comes to mind. As the work progressed it became apparent that the critical impasse was triadic. Isabel had been her father's favourite over an older sister. Despite her considerable intelligence and ability, she had held herself back out of a combination of guilt and fear: guilt that she was getting what her sister was not and fear of the retribution which would follow from this. At the same time the price she was paying in order to remain her father's 'little girl' needed to be addressed.

Contemporary systemic practice takes us back to the social constructionist ideas we addressed in Chapter 1. Karl Tomm, who had some contact with Fritz Perls, has taken forward the narrative approach of Michael White and David Epston (1990) in the form of what he terms 'internalised other interviewing' (Tomm, Hoyt, & Madigan, 1998). The psychological self is seen as being made up of an internalised community and the patterns of interactions between members of that community. The intention is to uncover the subjective assumptions and embodied knowledge that organises the client's engagement with the world.

Conclusion

In this chapter we have focused on a relational theme which can emerge in the challenge we face in establishing ourselves as autonomous individuals. As we have seen, this is under-pinned by our earliest experiences of separation and individuation. In less than optimal circumstances, Mark had come to find a semblance of autonomy in the rejection of other people. The solution to his dilemma had been to say 'no', which left him unable to engage productively with the world by acknowledging and pursuing what he wanted. This called for a response from the therapist which was both robust and creative. By its nature, autonomy cannot be given but has to be fought for. The therapist's task was to challenge Mark's thin narrative of rejection of others and rejection by them. Intervention could have been informed by any number of theories and models. Here, we have focused primarily on ego-state analysis as providing a useful map, serving to keep us away from dangerous ter-ritory. In the process of this, Mark came to find his power in the context of a relationship.

8   The Therapeutic Encounter: A Safe Emergency

In a dialogue between Gregory Bateson and Carl Rogers which took place in Marin College, California in 1975 the two exponents of very different philosophical and theoretical positions reached a point of agreement in a shared critique of behavioural therapy as it was practised at the time. Rogers recounted a visit of observation he had made to the state hospital:

> I was amazed at what happened when the patient came in. He was greeted by 'Oh John I haven't seen you since last week'. There was a most caring and welcoming atmosphere as they ushered him into his little cubicle to do his monkey business with the machine. (Kirschenbaum & Henderson, 1990, p. 187)

It is now well-established that the quality of the emotional connection between client and therapist is of greater significance in positive outcome than the therapist's theoretical orientation. This is not to be taken as an invitation to give up on theory in favour of some ill-defined way of relating which is taken to be 'therapeutic'. Theory has a place in that it provides an alternative to the world-taken-for-granted of common culture, challenging the common-sense and allowing for the counter-intuitive. Our proposal has been that you should value your theory but, at the same time, you need to know it for what it is: a partial attempt to account for the complexities of the human condition and one that has a tendency to construct the world on its own terms (Warhus, 2001). We need to keep in mind Gregory Bateson's assertion that the map is not the territory.

At the same time, there are general principles which follow from the nature of being human. The human animal enters the world incomplete and depends on another to finish the job. It is through relationship that we find out who we are, form views of others and take a place in the world. We all face the tension between belonging and autonomy, and each of us needs to find a balance between intimacy and control. Developmentally, our task is to connect to the other, establish a role in the group and take a place in the world. In our management of this we give meaning to experience through the construction of a story or narrative which is enacted in social performance.

When the client arrives at your consulting room the expectations of both parties are met by the client providing an account of the troubles that have brought them to your door. As we have seen, the story is not just told: it is also performed with accompanying gestures. In this sense the therapeutic encounter is a dramatic event with the therapist allocated a role in the play. We have proposed that they should take the part initially with good grace. The productive way forward is to: take note of the counter-transference; be inducted into the system; acknowledge and articulate the client's frame of reference. To do otherwise would not only be impolite but is an invitation to resistance. As we have argued in Chapter 3, it is a therapeutic error to consider resistance to be a property of the client. More accurately, it is a function of the therapist's failure to appreciate the significance of the client's performance as a survival strategy. It is no exaggeration to suggest that this has come out of circumstances which for the client were a matter of life and death. It follows that forging a relationship with the client is not a simple matter of making a warm engagement where 'one size fits all'. It requires that the therapist respect the client's fortitude and creativity in finding a way through the vicissitudes of early life and for keeping themselves in good-enough shape to have made it to the session. Here, the therapist needs to communicate a profound appreciation of the client's solution that has since become problematic.

Persistence and resistance

The clients we have met in previous chapters are each living out their own unreflected-upon tragic journey. Despite their unique and complex stories, each has one thing in common: they all find themselves persisting in patterns of relating which have become disadvantageous. For example, Tony in Chapter 2 would consistently walk out of jobs and relationships just when he had a chance of making them a success. In Chapter 5, Lucy found herself in an endless cycle of attempting to please others at her own expense in order to win their love and affection. In turn this left her feeling increasingly rageful as her own needs were left unmet. Similarly, in Chapter 6, we saw how Rebecca kept others at bay through her critical and grandiose attitude and subsequently was increasingly confronted with the terror of isolation.

Theoretical accounts of these phenomena have been referred to and developed throughout the book. In Chapter 2, we saw how Tony engaged in a 'repetition' of his sudden eviction from the family by the re-staging of this drama in his sudden self-evictions from his work places and relationships. This was accounted for from within a psycho-analytic frame drawing on Freud's notion of 'repetition compulsion' (Freud, 1920). 'We repeat,' argued Freud, 'in order not to remember' (Freud, 1912, 1915). The pain of the rejection and perceived punishment at the hands of his parents constituted a trauma which Tony kept unconsciously repeating. In Chapter 5, we drew on game theory to account for the tendency to repeat unproductive patterns. Lucy's script decision was played out with the therapist as surrogate and her frame of reference confirmed as she re-enacted her old role in the parent dynamic and family system. Chapter 7 drew on ego-state analysis as a means to disrupt the minute-by-minute exchanges which keep the world predictable, opening the way to fresh possibilities. In Chapter 4, we outlined attachment theory and Bowlby's notion of 'attachment patterns' to help us understand Liz's avoidance of intimacy and connection to others. Within this model, attachment patterns become established as a result of infant–parent interactions and, in turn, they lead to the creation of 'internal working models'. 'Internal working models' represent the blueprints of the relationships between self and other which become internalised. These involve beliefs about what other people are like, how they are likely to behave towards us and give rise to a particular repertoire of emotional responses based on these predictions. We have drawn on 'object relations theory', both to shed light on Liz's rapprochement crisis and, in Chapter 6, in relation to Rebecca's annihilation of absent and unreliable parental figures from her internal world. The object relations tradition, characterised by Winnicott, Mahler and Kernberg, accounts for this type of repetition by proposing that when a child internalises the image of their significant others, they also take in the dynamics of that relationship. The psyche, it is argued, is governed by the dynamics present in our earliest experiences. Liz, for example, could not risk connecting because her internalised *other* was one who would control and take her over. Yet another account in Chapter 3 addresses the homeostatic tendency of systems: the way in which exchanges become circular and self-reinforcing, perpetuating the client's problematic place in the world. Here, we proposed the use of paradox and the therapeutic bind as a way of introducing something different in place of more of the same.

We have seen that models of therapy that privilege the relationship all have their own way of accounting for why and how people persist in repeating the very patterns of relating which are at the heart of their distress. All of these equally valid theoretical accounts of 'persistence', as coined by Lynne Hoffman (1993) were developed out of their authors' extensive encounters with adults in therapeutic settings. They deductively draw conclusions about the life and experiences of infants. To this body of knowledge we would wish to add some of the research findings which have arisen out of infant observation rather than out of hypothesised developmental pasts. Daniel Stern stands out within this literature as having made a profound contribution to our understanding of how babies experience their relational world (Stern, 1985, 2004; Stern, Sander, Nahum, Harrison, Lyons-Ruth, Morgan et al., 1998). Stern, and fellow researchers, introduced the concept of 'implicit relational knowing', which has the potential to offer a fresh approach to the familiar problem of persistence. Implicit relational knowing refers to the infant's, and subsequent adult's, implicit expectations of others that they will feel, respond and behave in particular ways. The central point of this concept is that infants operate on the basis of prediction.

A substantial body of research now suggests that infants possess a great deal of relational knowledge and use this to predict and anticipate responses from their mothers. Stern argues that infants become upset and unsettled when their mothers respond in unexpected ways that veer away from the established implicit rules of engagement which the infant has 'learned'. Infants have been shown to express anxiety when there is a surprise shift from an expected outcome. The type of *knowing* which Stern is describing is not one of which the client is conscious, yet it underpins all our interactions and informs 'how to be' with another (Stern, 1985). For the pre-verbal infant, this constitutes 'procedural' knowledge of relationships and is both out of awareness and not represented symbolically. Contemporary developments in the neuroscientific and attachment literature also point to the existence of phenomena captured in the concept of implicit relational knowledge. The infant's incomplete and immature brain is shaped and developed under the heavy influence of the mother's brain, and the emotional responses she provides to her infant are literally inscribed on his body (Cozolino, 2006; Fonagy, 2001; Gerhardt, 2004; Green, 2003).

One view is that human beings persist in understanding their relational world in particular ways because this constitutes their world-taken-for-granted. We relate in unique ways because we simply 'know' no other way. We bring coherence to our lived experience and construct particular narratives to help us explain and understand our world. To challenge these is to experience what Rollo May (1994) described as 'ontological anxiety'. The experience of having your version of reality shaken up is profoundly disconcerting and anxiety provoking. A distinction, or comparison, needs to be made between this type of resistance to change, one that resists entertaining different accounts about the world, and the psychoanalytic formulation of 'resistance'. The psychoanalytic client unconsciously chooses not to 'know' certain aspects of their relational world. This type of persistence is then one which can be defined as the client's unconscious distortion of reality in the quest of the avoidance of suffering. The person chooses not to confront aspects of experience despite unconsciously 'knowing' of their existence. These are important distinctions as they have implications for the nature of 'resistance'.

In either case, as clients we actively, if unconsciously, work against giving up our unique perspective on the world. We present for therapy requesting help and support with our distress. We are seldom willing, however, to consider alternative accounts of the origins of our suffering, less still are we willing to give up on long accustomed ways of being and engaging. We fend-off ideas presented to us which are incompatible with our chosen version of events. In addition, these persistent stories become enacted in the room as we attempt to enlist the therapist to confirm our frame of reference and join us in the act of repetition. We will provoke, seduce, cajole and, if necessary, attack the other in order for this confirmation to take place. All the clients encountered in this book presented their therapists with invitations to replay the very scenarios which were at the root of their distress. In this sense, *process* is the manifestation of persistence. Thus, the kind of help that we are consciously seeking normally comes in the guise of the therapist 'doing' or 'saying' something helpful which will make the pain and suffering go away. In other words, we are holding out for a 'magic wand'.

The notion of 'persistence' provides a different framing from the familiar notion of therapeutic 'resistance'. Our position is one which asserts that individuals persist in repeating old and dysfunctional relational patterns. Resistance, on the other hand, we see as being a function of a relationship irrespective of whether one conceptualises such resistance within a phenomenological or a psychoanalytic frame. We are arguing that resistance to therapeutic engagement or change is thus a relational problem. It can be understood as being co-constructed by therapist and client and best understood as a function of the therapist's inability to find a non-threatening way into the client's relational sphere.

A kind of loving

Our proposal is that in order to interrupt and challenge persistence we need to engage actively in the dramatic presentation of the client's story while drawing attention to the limitations of the account. In the face of the client's 'implicit relational knowing' we need to take the stance of a polite guest joining the population which already inhabits the client's internal and external worlds. At the same time, to be therapeutically effective we need to be prepared to be unpredictable. It should be kept in mind that there are two people engaged in this process and that we bring our own stories to the experience. These are not only therapeutic, in the form of theory, but also personal. The therapist brings their own implicit relational knowledge to the encounter. Therapeutic trainings do something towards helping us manage this. Probably the most useful of these is a requirement that trainees undertake their own therapy. With this, a group experience can be particularly useful. If properly led, the group exposes us to a range of emotional expression in a safe context.

While training and personal work will have had some limited impact, they do not render us immune to the dilemmas that have shaped our own place in the world. The principle of circularity reminds us that our clients will make as much impact upon us as we hope to have on them. We spend whole stretches of time shut in a confined space within which painful stories are told and powerful emotions expressed. This will inevitably trigger a response in us. We can find ourselves feeling inadequate, angry and inclined to do the least helpful thing – retreat from the client. This may take the obvious form of simply giving up on them. Therapeutic passivity provides more subtle variants. The therapist can find a number of ways of avoiding engaging in the relationship with the client. One way of making ourselves unavailable is by putting the theory before the client – they become a case rather than a person. This opens the way to building elegant conceptual constructions which provide fascinating accounts of the problem, preferably with references to obscure papers. Here, the therapist invests more emotional energy in their approach than in the client, apart from some irritation when they refuse to conform to the theory. At the other extreme, therapeutic passivity can show itself in mindless warm relating. While this gives every appearance of valuing the client, it misses the point by privileging a set of generalised relational principles over the complexities of the client's phenomenal world. Arguably, short of doing nothing at all, therapy takes its most passive form when process is reduced to procedure. Here, the encounter is rendered entirely safe by doggedly following a set of prescriptions laid down by the model. When the unpredictable shows itself it is neutralised by a distraction in the form of some kind of content-based activity. Timelines, geneograms and objective setting can be particularly helpful in keeping away the turmoil and uncertainty that arises when two human beings connect emotionally.

To be effective the therapist is required to bring sensitivity, good humour, playfulness and above all spontaneity to the therapeutic relationship. We will find ourselves unable to do this to the extent that we are immobilised by our own anger, fear and hurt. Further, clients will experience us as unavailable if we privilege philosophy, theory or methodology over a direct encounter with them. When the client's world-taken-for-granted is challenged in therapy and new horizons come into view, the level of anxiety experienced by clients increases. As we have seen, this can lead to a highly charged emotional climate in the consulting room and it is at this point that the therapist will need to be able to think, as well as respond emotionally. The framing we have provided of the therapist as a 'polite but unpredictable guest' should not be confused with an inability to provide consistent safety. Equally, unpredictability and the importance of subverting the transferential invitation should not be equated with any attempt to 'outmanoeuvre' the client. What we are arguing for here is a position that is absolutely on the side of the client.

At this point we should consider the aim of the therapeutic encounter. If one takes the view that as clients we are not in a position to 'know' what we need, as distinct from what we might want, then the question of aim becomes a tricky one. To say that as clients we are not always clear of what we need from therapy is not the same as saying that we do not have the major role in working out what that is. Once the idea of the 'magic wand' has been abandoned, therapy can be deemed to have truly started. This is often the work in itself. The commonplace assumption is that therapy is concerned with the alleviation of suffering. Although this is to some extent the case, a more realistic and ultimately more rewarding aim is one where the client learns, over time, to bear the full weight of their story to date. In other words, as Freud tells us, therapy involves learning to bear our difficult feelings rather than making them disappear.

Once confronted, the opportunity presents itself for the client to find a new, richer and ultimately more fulfilling solution to their conflicts than the ones they have relied upon since childhood. Liz, in Chapter 4, needed to take the risk of revealing aspects of herself to others in ways which she had never done before. Mark, in Chapter 7, had to take the risk of asking for what he wanted, of expressing his desire, and come out from behind the safety of refusal and lack of engagement. In the taking of these risks, clients will be confronted with long-hidden and avoided feelings of loss, shame, anxiety and rejection. These had been unbearable to date because the client, in infancy and childhood, lacked the type of containment in the form of an *other* who could help make these feelings understandable and survivable.

The therapist then needs to take up the mantle and stand in for the self-regulating other which was absent in early life (Stern, 1985). To say this is not to suggest that therapists should aim to provide some type of 're-parenting'. It is a poignant and important moment in any therapy when the client begins to mourn what was lacking from their experience of being parented. Holding out for the 'magic wand' can be understood as the client's persistent wish for the type of parenting which was not forthcoming in childhood. At times, however, the 'magic wand' desire represents the refusal to give up our childhood security, a type of unwillingness to confront the anxieties of adulthood.

To say that therapy is not a form of 're-parenting' does not mean that it should not aim to offer a reparative experience. Stern's 'self-regulating other' describes the role of the mother in organising the infant's early self-experience. Winnicott describes the 'mirror-role' performed by the mother in reflecting back to the infant an image of him- or herself. The infant sees in the mother's face the way in which he has altered her, and thus begins the process of constructing their sense of self (Winnicott, 1967). We are arguing that we find our *self* through our earliest intimate relations. What the infant sees reflected in his mother's eyes will inform who he believes himself to be. There is no self without other.

An integral part of this implicit process involves the mother's capacity to reflect back the infant's internal emotional experiences. This is a complex, yet intuitive process which requires the mother to be available to enter into the child's affective state in order to temporarily match it. If you've had the opportunity to care for a baby, cast your mind back to the experience of hearing the baby cry in the middle of the night. The volume, pitch and intensity of the cry will probably have the effect of getting even the most exhausted of parents out of bed. As you enter the nursery you yourself will be at a similar level of arousal or anxiety as that experienced by the baby. There is a sense of urgency that is provoked in us as a response to a baby's cry, and this mobilises us into action. The point is that by the time you come into contact with your baby, you are sharing an affective state. It is only from this position of synchronicity that you can begin to calm your baby down. It is the mother's own affect-regulating capacity that she brings to the aid of her infant. If, when woken by the crying baby, the mother falls into a rage she is unable to control or, conversely, feels a paralysing despair, she will not be available to help the baby return to a state of equilibrium. This describes the process of 'affect-regulation' discussed in the attachment and neuroscientific literature (Cozolino, 2002; Gerhardt, 2004; Stern, 1985). In time, the baby learns, as the mother once did, to carry out this function for him- or herself.

As our familiar ways of protecting ourselves from pain begin to be broken down in therapy, the therapist must be available to be recruited to carrying out this type of affect-regulation. In fact, the confrontation of long-avoided painful internal experiences, coupled with the presence of a benign and stable 'self-regulating other' is probably the key to the efficacy of psychotherapy. The therapist's subjectivity, his or her own internal world, must be brought into the relationship for the service of the client. It is only through this type of 'intersubjective' connection that the client may be in a position to begin to make his or her own internal world more bearable. As we have written about elsewhere, there is a world of difference between burdening the client with unhelpful self-disclosures and the lending of one's subjectivity for the client's therapeutic aims (Howard, 2008). What we are describing here is a kind of 'parental' loving through emotional attunement, affect-regulation and the co-construction of narratives. The contribution of attachment theory and neuroscience benefits from the addition of a social constructionist perspective (see Chapter 1). The suggestion that the self arises as a function of our perception of others' experience of us is a satisfying fit with the notion of mind as discourse or conversation (both verbal and non-verbal). The position is that meaning is not to be found in the mind of the individual but arises out of relationship with others. In this way meaning could be said to be generated in the client–therapist exchange (Warhus, 2001) with the therapist taking the role of 'significant other' in co-constructing a richer story.

To the extent that the therapist remains polite – accepts the transferential invitation; becomes inducted into the system; simply reflects the frame of reference; does nothing to disrupt the world-taken-for-granted – the client will experience the *safety* of the familiar as their 'implicit relational model' is confirmed. When the unexpected takes place an *emergency* presents itself. Cozolino (2002) draws upon Fritz Perls' notion of the 'safe emergency' to account for the therapeutic process by which clients are exposed to unintegrated and disregulating thoughts and feelings while held within a safe context and provided with the kind of nurturing experience which allows for integration. Perls set out to achieve this by deliberately constructing a dramatic event. Gestalt therapy traditionally takes the form of one-to-one therapy in a group. While the therapist draws on a number of active techniques to invite projection with a view to uncovering unconscious contents, the rest of the group function much as a Greek chorus, witnessing and commenting on the process. The general point here is that exposure to stress while contained in a supportive interpersonal context enhances the ability to tolerate emotional arousal. In one-to-one therapy, the therapist is required to perform all of these functions and through repetition the client internalises these skills and develops the capacity to self-regulate.

This work requires a contained yet engaged therapeutic other who is open to spontaneous emotional experience. Most of us implicitly carry out this function for our loved ones throughout life. The success of our adult intimate relationships often depends on a couple's ability to turn-take in this type of affect-regulation. Emotional spontaneity, however, is often the casualty of therapeutic training. As trainees we rightfully learn to be suspicious of commonplace ways of being helpful: reassurance, rescuing, over-identification and guidance. Essential though it may be to let go of these old and unhelpful ways of using our selves in the service of others, a by-product of developing this new way of 'being with' the other is that the intimacy of spontaneity and shared emotional experience is often lost.

The therapeutic stance and its implications for modalities

When presented with the way his ideas had been taken forward by others, Karl Marx famously declared '*Je ne suis pas Marxiste*' – I am not a Marxist. Why a German living in London should be writing in French belongs to a longer story, but the sentiment captures our position well. We are for intellectual rigor and sound practice, but we are against orthodoxy. There is now an unfortunate tendency to draw on the metaphor of 'tribe' to account for different traditions in the field of psychotherapy. This carries with it the connotation of culturally self-referential groupings. There is also a sub-text of tribal warfare. We have argued that theory should be valued. At the same time we might reflect upon how it comes about. An inspired and charismatic figure located in a particular cultural context provides a fresh take on the human condition and, in the process, engages in a debate with an existing dominant world-view. On the way, they pick up friends and disciples who take it upon themselves to spread the word. The new approach is required to define itself as what it is not: that which has gone on before. By the time these ideas have been passed on to the third or fourth generation, the world is not only a different place but history has been forgotten. The rich possibilities within which the original ideas were developed risk becoming a thin account defended with quasi-religious fervour.

In a seminal paper, Daniel Stern et al. (1998) make a convincing case for the 'more than' in challenging the psychoanalytic community to move beyond interpretation 'to special moments of person-to-person connection'. A 'more than' presents itself to each of our modalities. It is to be found both in that which does not fit within the tribal culture and by drawing upon common principles of human relatedness: narrative and enactment. We have set out to draw attention to theories and models which account for the construction of narrative and its enactment in the therapeutic encounter. It requires us to uncover the embedded and be open to the other.

As well as launching the professions of counselling and psychotherapy into existence, psychoanalysis has made, and continues to make, a profound and lasting contribution to our understanding of human nature. It has irrevocably entered the public and cultural psyche, and psychoanalytic terminology now peppers our daily language.

The role of meaning attribution, interpretation and insight, which are at the heart of the psychoanalytic project, are generally accepted as a helpful and integral part of successful therapeutic experiences. To be at the receiving end of an astute interpretation, uncomfortable though it may be, allows us to feel profoundly understood. More importantly, it allows us to begin to understand ourselves in new and important ways. However, research has shown that, as any psychodynamic therapist will recognise, it is a common experience for clients (such as Liz in Chapter 4) to find that insight alone is not enough for change to ensue. This assertion often leads to discussions around the timing of interpretations (Stern et al., 1998), suggesting that only when the client is 'ready' can the interpretation become a catalyst for change. Similarly, it is generally understood that intellectual insight alone is not generative but that it is the coupling of ideas and their corresponding affect which will provide the vehicle for psychological change.

This emphasis on interpretation and the neutrality epitomised by the analytic stance have, at times, meant that psychodynamic practitioners tend towards adopting a fairly passive stance. Yet when we consider the work of some of psychoanalysis' founding fathers and mothers, we see clinicians who did not simply have insights to offer their clients but who engaged in strategic, creative practices. Winnicott's unfailingly championing the side of young mothers in his clinical case studies showed him making strategic interventions in ways which would not now be considered strictly psychoana-lytic (Winnicott, 1975). Sandor Ferenczi challenged the established norms of the time by advocating the use of 'active' strategies within the therapeutic encounter. He famously asked an opera singer client with performance anxiety to 'perform' during her sessions (Rachman, 2007). Similarly, accounts provided by Freud's patients describe him as refreshingly less than Freudian. The point here is that the origins of psychoanalysis alluded to the need for what Stern et al. (1998) called 'something more' than interpretation.

Let us return to the notion of persistence. Psychodynamic practitioners will easily recognise this phenomenon as referring to *transference*. This represents the manner in which clients communicate their earliest experiences through the way they engage, or fail to engage, with their therapists. There is a general tendency to think of transference as an attempt at communication. Transference, in this classical sense, is then a distorted communication of unconscious, unresolved conflict. If, however, we can expand the definition of transference to take into account the notion of *implicit relational knowing*, then we can begin to see that the client's way of being with his therapist represents the history and limits of his relational experience. In order to expand our relational experi-ence, psychological *acts* are needed in addition to psychological *information* by way of interpretation (Stern et al., 1998).

If we look back at Chapter 2, we see that the therapist used her growing sense of inadequacy provoked by Tony's demands in order to express that she genuinely didn't have any answers to his pressing questions. Her willingness to reveal this and yet still be up for doing the work helped Tony overcome his fear of failure and rejection and had the effect of by-passing his resistance to beginning the work. We can assume that her 'interpretation' of his controlling behaviour would probably have had very little effect at best, and at worst brought about an even greater need to control.

As we saw in Chapter 1, the therapist as 'Deus ex Machina' has the task to enrich, expand and alter the client's relational map. Meaning attribution, by way of insight or interpretation, has an important place as it helps to reconfigure the client's conceptu-alisations of their internal world. When the therapist responds in a manner which chal-lenges the client's *implicit relational knowledge*, crucially from *within* the relationship, or in other words, subverts the transferential invitation, a type of crisis ensues. The world-taken-for-granted is suspended and a reconfiguration of the relational sphere is sud-denly on the cards. This type of activity is not one which will be best carried out by the largely silent, passive therapist, but requires the same level of aliveness and engagement that we would all hope an infant might find in the eyes of the other. We are, of course, not talking here about a lack of containment or of unhelpful self-disclosure but of a willingness to be creative, flexible, surprising and, above all, human.

Those taking a person-centred position will find much in this book which is familiar to them. At they same time they may have visited unfamiliar territory, and perhaps some aspects are completely foreign. As we have seen, some approaches which come into this category require the therapist to be active. The emphasis on the therapeutic relationship will come as no surprise to the humanistic practitioners. For Carl Rogers the relationship is the therapy, and there is much to value in the 'kind of loving' implicit in the communication of the core conditions, since these have something of the qualities associated with a secure attachment in early life. From a neuroscientific point of view they provide an excellent antidote to shame, opening the way to the experience of warmth and acceptance which, in turn, stimulates the very biochemical exchanges that enhance socio-emotional learning. As we have seen, the client brings to the relationship their 'implicit relational knowing' and invites the therapist to join them in their world-taken-for-granted. To the extent that the therapist remains authentic and congruent, this 'transferential invitation' will not stick and the client's 'frame of reference' will be challenged. In conditions of safety, an emergency arises from the failure of the therapist to conform to expectations.

While the person-centred approach can account for transference, it lacks an explicit framework within which it can be understood and managed. There is 'one size' and it must 'fit all'. The client will inevitably bring much more energy to bear on maintaining the frame of reference upon which their survival has depended than the therapist can ever hope to match. The adage might be: take care of the congruence and the transference will take care of itself. Our suggestion is that if you understand the distortions of the frame of reference manifest in the transference, you are better placed to be authentic. The notions of 'conditions of worth' and 'self-concept' have considerable value. The 'more than' can be found in the detail and specificity available in accounts of human growth and development. The notion of empathy can be ill-defined at the risk of trainees and practitioners taking it to be no more than an unregulated and indiscriminate expression of warmth. You may recall how the therapist nearly came unstuck with Michael in Chapter 3. In the therapist's attempt to understand the climate of the client's world, empathic expression needs to be conducted in a way that is sensitive to the level of emotion the client can handle. A sunny disposition can be deeply infuriating, if not downright terrifying, to a client who brings a lifetime's experience of being 'out in the rain', 'subject to fierce thunderstorms' or 'frozen with fear'. The child psychologist Dan Hughes (2007) uses the term 'loud empathy' to account for a response which replicates the affect-regulating exchanges between mother and child we encountered earlier in this chapter. The therapist matches the intensity and rhythm of the client's affect.

A word about catharsis. The powerful expression of emotion has a place in therapy, but it needs to be approached with some care since it does not necessarily indicate that anything productive is taking place. Repetition-compulsion and game theory invite us to treat cathartic expression with caution. Personal development groups are a feature of trainings, and we have argued that they have some considerable merit if well led. With poor leadership, they can be disastrous. Group members with easy access to anger become furious in the opening moments of the group. The fearful become terrified. Others feel sad about this unfortunate turn of events, while the rest find themselves shamed by the whole thing. An effective group leader will bring this to the group's attention. If the leader remains passive, all that will have happened is that the group members' expectations will have been confirmed.

We have already referred to the way in which training, while necessary, has the potential to damage emotional spontaneity. This takes a particularly pernicious form when principles are taught as methodology and reduced to skills. Survivors of such trainings, usually at an introductory level, have internalised a set of instructions and proscriptions without a grasp of their philosophical and theoretical underpinnings. Frozen by a semi-mystical belief in the sanctity of the 'relationship', the majority of their interventions take the form of a slavish repetition of the client's statements. Questions must never be asked (though trainees quickly find a way round this through endless 'wondering'). Every reference to 'you' is greeted by an invitation to make an 'I' statement. There is even an acronym for how non-verbal communication is to be conducted – SOLER (Sit squarely, Open posture, Lean towards the client, Eye contact, Relax). Another feature of skills training is practice with silences. Trainees can come to confuse respect for the client with doing nothing. If the relationship is the vehicle for change, both therapist and client must have a presence. When the client overloads the therapist with content, brooking no interruption while the therapist remains 'respectfully' silent, there are two passive people in the room and no relationship is taking place.

There are sound reasons for much of this, as the client is to be encouraged to frame the world in their own unique manner. The common-sense idea that asking questions somehow arrives at solutions needs to be addressed. Non-verbal or analogical communication requires attention since it has primary significance in an emotional exchange. A return to principles reminds us that authenticity, spontaneity, creativity and above all humanity are central to working directly with process in the therapeutic exchange. None of these are to be found in the enactment of tribal rituals.

References

Ainsworth, M. (1967). *Infancy in Uganda: Infant Care and the Growth of Love*. Baltimore, MD: Johns Hopkins University Press.

Ainsworth, M. & Bowlby, J. (1965). *Child Care and the Growth of Love*. London: Penguin.

Ainsworth, M., Blehar, M.C., Waters, E. & Wall, S. (1978). *Patterns of Attachment: A Psychological Study of the Strange Situation*. Hillsdale, NJ: Erlbaum.

Allen, D. (1988). *Unifying Individual and Family Therapies*. San Francisco, CA: Jossey-Bass.

Auerswald, E. (1985). Thinking about thinking in family therapy. *Family Process, 24,* 1, 1–12.

Bachelard, G. (1958). *The Poetics of Space*. New York: Orion Press.

Bandler, R. & Grinder, J. (1975). *The Structure of Magic I*. Palo Alto, CA: Science and Behavior Books Inc.

Bandler, R. & Grinder, J. (1976). *The Structure of Magic II*. Palo Alto, CA: Science and Behavior Books Inc.

Bateson, G. (1971). A systems approach. *International Journal of Psychiatry, 9,* 242–244.

Bateson, G., Jackson, D.D., Haley, J. & Weakland, J. (1956). Toward a theory of schizophrenia. *Behavioral Science, 1,* 251–264.

Becker, W.S. (1963). *Outsiders: Studies in the Sociology of Deviance*. New York: The Free Press.

Berger, P.L. & Luckmann, T. (1967). *The Social Construction of Reality*. New York: Anchor.

Berne, E. (1961). *Transactional Analysis in Psychotherapy*. New York: Grove Press.

Berne, E. (1966). *Principles of Group Treatment* (p. 364). New York: Open University Press.

Best, S. & Kellner, D. (1991). *Postmodern Theory: Critical Interrogations*. New York: Guilford Press.

Bott, D. (1988). A process model of developmental failure and associated pathology. *British Psychological Society*, Counselling Section Review, *3*(1), 25–35.

Bott, D. (1994). A family systems framework for intervention with individuals. *Counselling Psychology Quarterly, 7*(2).

Bowlby, J. (1969). Attachment and Loss: Volume 1: Attachment. *The International Psycho-Analytical Library, 79,* 1–401. London: The Hogarth Press and the Institute of Psycho-Analysis.

Bowlby, J. (1979). *The Making and Breaking of Emotional Bonds*. London: Routledge.

Bowlby, J. (1988). *A Secure Base*. London: Routledge.

Cicero, M.T. (1817). *Tuscalan Disputations* (trans. by C.D. Jonge). Harpers New Classical Library. New York: Harper Brothers.

Clarkson, P. (1992). *Transactional Analysis Psychotherapy: An Integrated Approach.* London: Routledge.

Cozolino, L. (2002). *The Neuroscience of Psychotherapy: Building and Rebuilding the Human Brain.* New York: Norton.

Cozolino, L. (2006). *The Neuroscience of Human Relationships: Attachment and the Developing Social Brain.* New York: Norton.

Dare, C. (1981). Psychoanalysis and family therapy. In S. Walrond-Skinner (Ed.), *Developments in Family Therapy.* Balmain: Law Book Co. of Australasia.

Derrida, J. (1974). *Of Grammatology.* Baltimore, MD: Johns Hopkins University Press.

Erikson, E. (1965). *Childhood and Society.* London: Hogarth Press.

Erskine, R. (2003). Introjection, psychic presence and Parent ego-state. In C. Sills & H. Hargaden (Eds.), *Ego-states.* Richmond: Worth.

Fairbairn, W.R.D. (1952). *Psychological Studies of Personality.* London: Routledge and Keegan Paul.

Fink, B. (1999). *A Clinical Introduction to Lacanian Psychoanalysis: Theory and Technique.* Cambridge, MA: Harvard University Press.

Fonagy, P. (2001). *Attachment Theory and Psychoanalysis.* New York: Other Press.

Foucault, M. (1975). *Discipline and Punish: The Birth of the Prison.* New York: Random House.

Freud, S. & Breuer, J. (1895). *Studies on Hysteria. Standard Edition of the Complete Psychological Works of Sigmund Freud, Vol. II* (1893–1895) (pp. xxix–xxx). London: Vintage Classics.

Freud, S. (1909). Notes upon a case of obessional neurosis (the rat man). *Standard Edition of the Complete Works of Sigmund Freud, Vol. X* (pp. 151–249). London: Vintage Classics.

Freud, S. (1912). The dynamics of the transference. *The Standard Edition of the Complete Psychological Works of Sigmund Freud, Vol. XII.* London: Vintage Classics.

Freud, S. (1914a). On narcissism. *The Standard Edition of the Complete Psychological Works of Sigmund Freud, Volume XIV (1914–1916): On the History of the Psycho-Analytic Movement, Papers on Metapsychology and Other Works* (pp. 67–102). London: Vintage Classics.

Freud, S. (1914b). Remembering, repeating and working-through (further recommendations on the technique of psycho-analysis II). *The Standard Edition ofthe Complete Psychological Works of Sigmund Freud, Volume XII (1911–1913): The Case of Schreber, Papers on Technique and Other Works* (pp. 145–156). London: Vintage Classics.

Freud, S. (1915). Observations on transference love. *The Standard Edition of the Complete Psychological Works of Sigmund Freud, Vol. XII.* London: Vintage Classics.

Freud, S. (1920). Beyond the pleasure principle. *The Standard Edition of the Complete Psychological Works of Sigmund Freud, Volume XVIII (1920–1922): Beyond the Pleasure Principle, Group Psychology and Other Works* (pp. 1–64). London: Vintage Classics.

Freud, S. (1923). *The Ego and the Id. Standard Edition of the Complete Works of Sigmund Freud, XIX* (p. 23). London: Vintage Classics.

Freud, S. (1924). The dissolution of the Oedipus complex. *The Standard Edition of the Complete Psychological Works of Sigmund Freud, Volume XIX (1923–1925): The Ego and the Id and Other Works* (pp. 171–180). London: Vintage Classics.

Freud, S. (1926). Inhibitions, symptoms and anxiety. *The Standard Edition of the Complete Psychological Works of Sigmund Freud, Volume XX (1925–1926): An Autobiographical Study, Inhibitions, Symptoms and Anxiety, The Question of Lay Analysis and Other Works* (pp. 75–176). London: Vintage Classics.

Freud, S. (1930). Civilization and its discontents. *The Standard Edition of the Complete Psychological Works of Sigmund Freud, Volume XXI (1927–1931): The Future of an Illusion, Civilization and its Discontents, and Other Works* (pp. 57–146). London: Vintage Classics.

Gergen, K. (1999). *An Invitation to Social Constructionism.* London: Sage.

Gergen, K. (2008). Therapeutic challenges of multi-being. *Journal of Family Therapy, 30*(4), 335–349.

Gerhardt, S. (2004). *Why Love Matters: How Affection Shapes a Baby's Brain.* London: Routledge.

Goffman, E. (1956). *The Presentation of Self in Everyday Life.* New York: Anchor.

Goffman, E. (1961). *Asylums: Essays on the Social Situation of Mental Patients and Other Inmates.* New York: Doubleday.

Goffman, E. (1963). *Stigma: Notes on the Management of Spoiled Identity.* Englewood Cliffs, NJ: Prentice-Hall.

Green, V. (Ed.). (2003). *Emotional Development in Psychoanalysis, Attachment Theory and Neuroscience: Making Connections.* New York: Brunner-Routledge.

Guttman, H. (1991). Systems theory, cybernetics and epistemology. In A. Gurman & D. Kniskern (Eds.), *Handbook of Family Therapy,* Vol. 2. New York: Brunner/Mazel.

Haley, J. (1969). The art of being a failure as a therapist. *American Journal of Orthopsychiatry, 39*(4), 691–695.

Haley, J. (1973). *Uncommon Therapy: The Psychiatric Techniques of Milton H. Erickson, M.D.* New York: Grune & Stratton.

Haley, J. (1976). *Problem Solving Therapy.* San Francisco, CA: Jossey-Bass.

Haley, J. (1980). *Leaving Home.* New York: Mcgraw-Hill.

Heller, J. (1994). *Catch-22.* London: Vintage.

Hoffman, L. (1993). *Exchanging Voices: A Collaborative Approach to Family Therapy.* London: Karnac.

Howard, P. (2008). Psychoanalytic Psychotherapy. In S. Paul & S. Haugh (Eds.), *The Therapeutic Relationship.* London: Process Press.

Hughes, D. (2007). *Attachment Focused Family Therapy.* New York: Norton.

Jenkins, H. & Asen, K. (1992). Family therapy without the family: a framework for systemic practice. *Journal of Family Therapy, 14,* 1–14.

Kahler, T. (1975). Driver the key to the process script. *Transactional Analysis Journal, 5*(3), 280–284.

Karpman, S. (1968). Fairy tales and script drama analysis. *Transactional Analysis Bulletin, 7*(26), 39–43.

Kernberg, O. (1965). Notes on countertransference. *Journal of the American Psychoanalytic Association, 13,* 38–56.

Kernberg, O.F. (1970). Factors in the psychoanalytic treatment of narcissistic personalities. *Journal of the American Psychoanalytic Association, 18*, 51–85.

Kernberg, O.F. (1974). Contrasting viewpoints regarding the nature and psychoanalytic treatment of narcissistic personalities: a preliminary communication. *Journal of the American Psychoanalytic Association, 22*, 255–267.

Kirschenbaum, H. & Henderson, V. (Eds.). (1990). *Carl Rogers Dialogues.* London: Constable.

Kohut, H. (1966). Forms and transformations of narcissism. *Journal of the American Psychoanalytic Association, 14*, 243–272.

Kohut, H. (1968). The psychoanalytic treatment of narcissistic personality disorders. *Psychoanalytic Study of the Child, 23*, 86–113.

Kohut, H. (1971). *The Analysis of the Self.* New York: International Universities Press.

Kohut, H. (1977). *The Restoration of the Self.* New York: International Universities Press.

Lacan, J. (1949). The mirror stage as formative of the function of the I as revealed in psychoanalytic experience. In B. Fink (Trans.), *Ecrits: A Selection* (2004). New York: Norton.

Lacan, J. (2004). *Ecrits: A Selection.* B. Fink (Trans.). New York: Norton.

Lewin, K. (1951) *Field Theory in Social Science: Selected Theoretical Papers.* D. Cartwright (Ed.). New York: Harper & Row.

Lewis, H.B. (1971). Shame and guilt in neurosis. *Psychoanalytic* Review, 58, 419–438.

Lewis, M. (1992). *Shame: The Exposed Self.* New York: The Free Press.

Lyotard, J. (1979). *The Postmodern Conditition: A Report on Knowledge.* Manchester: Manchester University Press.

Mahler, M.S., Pine, F. & Bergman, A. (1975). *The Psychological Birth of the Human Infant: Symbiosis and Individuation.* New York: Basic Books.

May, R. (1994). Contributions of existential psychotherapy. In R. May, E. Angel & H. Ellenberg (Eds.), *Existence.* London: Jason Aronson.

McLeod, J. (1997). *Narrative and Psychotherapy.* London: Sage.

McNeel, J. (1976). The parent interview. *Transactional Analysis Journal, 6*(1), 61–68.

Mead, G.H. (1934). *Mind, Self, and Society.* Chicago, IL: Chicago University Press.

Minuchin, S. (1976). *Families and Family Therapy.* Cambridge, MA: Harvard University Press.

Mollon, P. (1993). *The Fragile Self: The Structure of Narcissistic Disturbance.* London: Whurr.

Nichols, M. (1987). *The Self in the System.* New York: Brunner/Mazel.

Rachman, A.W. (2007). Sandor Ferenczi's contributions to the evolution of psychoanalysis. *Psychoanalytic Psychology, 24*, 74–96.

Rogers, C. (1951). *Client-centered Therapy: Its Current Practice, Implications and Theory.* London: Constable.

Rycroft, C. (1968). *A Critical Dictionary of Psychoanalysis.* Harmondsworth: Penguin.

Sarup, M. (1993). *An Introductory Guide to Poststructuralism and Postmodernism* (2nd ed.). Harlow: Harvester Wheatsheaf.

Schiff, J., Mellor, K., Richman, D., Fishman, J., Wolz, L. & Mombe, D. (1975). *The Cathexis Reader: Transactional Analysis Treatment of Psychosis.* New York: Harper Row.

Spence, D. & Wallerstein, R. (1982). *Narrative Truth and Historical Truth: Meaning and Interpretation in Psychoanalysis*. New York: Norton.

Steiner, C. (1974). *Scripts People Live*. New York: Grove.

Stern, D. (1985). *The Interpersonal World of the Infant: A View from Psychoanalysis and Developmental Psychology*. New York: Basic Books.

Stern, D. (2004). *The Present Moment in Psychotherapy and Everyday Life*. New York: Norton.

Stern, D.N., Sander, L.W., Nahum, J.P., Harrison, A.M., Lyons-Ruth, K., Morgan, A.C., Bruschweilerstern, N. & Tronick, E.Z. (1998). Non-interpretive mechanisms in psychoanalytic therapy: the 'something more' than interpretation. *International Journal of Psychoanalysis, 79*, 903–921.

Stewart, I. & Joines, V. (1987) *TA Today: A New Introduction to Transactional Analysis*. Derby: Lifespace.

Symington, N. (1993). *Narcissism: A New Theory*. London: Karnac.

Tomm, K., Hoyt, M. & Madigan, S. (1998) Honoring our internalized others and the ethics of caring: a conversation with Karl Tomm. In M. Hoyt (Ed.), *The Handbook of Constructive Therapies* (pp. 198–218). (Republished in *Interviews with Brief Therapy Experts*, Brunner-Routledge, Philadelphia, pp. 245–264, 2001.)

Wampold, B. (2001). *The Great Psychotherapy Debate*. New York: Earlbaum.

Ware, P. (1983). Personality adaptions (doors to therapy). *Transactional Analysis Journal, 13*(1).

Warhus, L. (2001). Therapy: a social construction. In K.J. Gergen (Ed.), *Social Construction in Context*. London: Sage.

Watzlawick, P., Beavin, J. & Jackson, D. (1967). *Pragmatics of Human Communication*. New York: Norton.

Weeks, R. & L'Abate, L. (1982). *Paradoxical Psychotherapy: Theory and Practice with Individuals, Couples, and Families*. New York: Brunner/Mazel.

White, M. & Epston, D. (1990). *Narrative Means to Therapeutic Ends*. New York: Norton.

Wiener, N. (1954). *Cybernetics or Control and Communication in the Animal and the Machine* (2nd ed.). Cambridge, MA: Massachussets Institute of Technology Press.

Winnicott, D. (1971). *Playing and Reality*. London: Routledge.

Winnicott, D.W. (1965). The maturational processes and the facilitating environment: studies in the theory of emotional development. *The International Psycho-Analytical Library, 64*, 1–276. London: The Hogarth Press and the Institute of Psycho-Analysis.

Winnicott, D.W. (1967). Mirror-role of the mother and family in child development. In P. Lomas (Ed.), *The Predicament of the Family: A Psycho-Analytical Symposium* (pp. 26–33). London: Hogarth.

Winnicott, D.W. (1975). Through paediatrics to psycho-analysis. *The International Psycho-Analytical Library, 100*, 1–325. London: The Hogarth Press and the Institute of Psycho-Analysis.

Index

Page numbers in **bold** indicate main discussion.